FRONT DESK
Security and Safety

An On-the-Job Guide to Handling Emergencies, Threats, and Unexpected Situations

Betty A. Kildow, CBCP, FBCI

AMACOM

American Management Association

New York • Atlanta • Brussels • Chicago • Mexico City • San Francisco
Shanghai • Tokyo • Toronto • Washington, D.C.

Special discounts on bulk quantities of AMACOM books are available to corporations, professional associations, and other organizations. For details, contact Special Sales Department, AMACOM, a division of American Management Association, 1601 Broadway, New York, NY 10019.
Tel.: 212-903-8316. Fax: 212-903-8083.
Web Site: www.amacombooks.org

This publication is designed to provide accurate and authoritative information in regard to the subject matter covered. It is sold with the understanding that the publisher is not engaged in rendering legal, accounting, or other professional service. If legal advice or other expert assistance is required, the services of a competent professional person should be sought.

Library of Congress Cataloging-in-Publication Data

Kildow, Betty A.
   Front desk security and safety : an on-the-job guide to handling emergencies, threats, and unexpected situations / Betty A. Kildow.—1st ed.
        p. cm.
Includes bibliographical references and index.
   ISBN 0-8144-0826-5
 1. Emergency management. I. Title.
   HD49.K54 2003
   658.4'7—dc22

                                                      2003015770

Printing number

10 9 8 7 6 5 4 3 2 1

CONTENTS

ACKNOWLEDGMENTS

This book was written with the goal of providing essential knowledge of emergency management for front desk professionals and helping them and others fulfill ongoing or newly-assigned emergency management responsibilities. For many, these responsibilities are an additional hat to wear, one that is not included in the formal job description. Other front desk professionals have seen a need for a more proactive approach to addressing safety and security issues and stepped forward to fill the void. In either case, emergency management responsibilities often come with little guidance on how to best perform the required duties, and there is frequently a lack of understanding about how the front desk's response to emergency situations fits into the organization's bigger picture.

I have heard it said that an expert is a person who knows enough about a subject to know she doesn't know everything but doesn't admit it, at least not out loud. And so it is as we prepare to respond to safety and security threats, emergencies, and disasters. While we all continue to learn, few are absolute experts. Just when we think we may have a handle on things, the world rotates and shifts and we are faced with a whole new set of vulnerabilities that force a re-examination of our approach to emergency management. The positive side of this picture is that this continually changing environment keeps us moving forward and develops more experience, greater knowledge, and better prepared organizations and people.

I would not be so bold as to call myself an expert (and am a bit leery of anyone who would opt to self-bestow that title). I will readily admit out loud that I do not know everything there is to know about safety, security, and emergency management. What I have done in this book is to share the things I *do* know as a result of working in this field for the past fifteen years. In addition to formal education, my colleagues, experience, and even a bit of trial and error have been my teachers. I am pleased to be able to pass along to others my lessons learned.

My hope is that each person who reads this book will find value in the content, now and in the future, as he takes on an increasingly larger role in preparing for and responding to emergencies, threats, and unexpected situations.

Many people have directly and indirectly contributed to making this book possible.

An acknowledgment to my colleagues and friends in the emergency management and business continuity profession, in particular Barbara Foster who first opened the door for me, John Laye for his encouragement and trust, and Anne Warren, a fellow native Hoosier, for her support.

Thank you to each of the people and organizations with whom I have an opportunity to work. Many of you have become friends as we have worked together through the challenges developing emergency management and business continuity plans for your organizations. I am grateful for your confidence in me.

My appreciation and thanks to Christina McLaughlin, my editor at AMACOM, first for offering me the opportunity to write this book, and then for providing indispensable support, guidance, and wonderful ideas and suggestions. You worked miracles. Big thank you's to Renita Hanfling for first recognizing the need for a book on this topic and to Mike Sivilli for watching over the project while it was in production.

A warm thank you in appreciation to my wonderful, much too far away family, all of whom give me reason to remember that life, with all of its trials and troubles, is good. For Wyatt. For Kent (Thank you for never letting me forget it was possible, Kent.) For Terry whose constant encouragement, support, and patience with this endeavor, as with all others over the years, gave me the confidence to set out on yet another new adventure and then get the job done. And for Annaleise and Sebastian, may we all always lead you to a place where you'll be safe.

With deep gratitude to my parents who by their example have taught us all the true meaning of love and of courage.

INTRODUCTION

The Importance of the Front Desk in the Organization's Safety and Security Program

Whether your front desk is a security desk in the lobby of a high-rise building, an elaborate reception area in a large corporate office, a multitasking desk near the entry of a small office, or a customer service counter, the people staffing that desk represent the organization to everyone who comes in the front door. You meet, greet, screen, direct, soothe, and address the myriad needs of customers, clients, vendors, contractors, sales representatives, delivery people, service people, and others who approach the front desk throughout the day. You are an ambassador while handling with aplomb and grace the problems and minor emergencies that present themselves on a daily basis.

In addition, you are now being asked to take an increasingly important role in protecting the safety and well-being of the people in your building and the organization's physical assets. You are the eyes and ears that notice when something seems amiss, a person's actions are suspect, or a package looks as though it doesn't belong in the building. You are also the person to whom visitors to your building, and often fellow employees, turn for direction and help when there is an emergency of any type, minor or major.

The Changing Face of Safety and Security

The World Trade Center and Pentagon attacks, threats to health including severe acute respiratory syndrome (SARS), anthrax and the possibility of other biological attacks, dirty bomb attacks, and the increasing number of violent workplace incidents have forced organizations to reevaluate their safety and security plans. This book addresses the increasingly complex and challenging role of the front desk in the organization's overall emergency preparedness and response efforts. It provides basic training for those new to safety and security responsibilities and will serve as a refresher and provide an update for those with more experience. Procedures for handling emergencies that were not even on our radar screen just a few short years ago are included. We have learned that previously unheard-of and unbelievable disasters can, and do, happen. While the majority of the emergencies to which you will be called upon to respond will be minor—an employee or visitor illness or minor injury or perhaps a building evacuation as a result of a small fire—it is no longer reasonable to presume immunity to major catastrophes like those we all too often see in newspapers and on television newscasts. We have a new reality. As a result, we must take a new look at our organization's safety and security measures and the related responsibilities of the front desk professional to make certain we are prepared for the emergencies we have faced in the past, today's new threats, and any currently unknown hazards that may arise in the future.

While awareness and preparedness are essential, it is equally important that we not live in fear, but rather take the steps necessary to meet the needs of our time. Review your existing plans and procedures to see if they provide the guidance needed to address today's challenges. Change to meet the times with plan enhancements and additions that will help ensure that all possible threats to the safety and well-being of employees and visitors to your location are addressed. Take every opportunity to educate yourself and participate in training that raises your preparedness to the highest possible level.

If your organization has not yet established a comprehensive emergency management program, talk with management about beginning the process now. Volunteer to work with representatives of other departments, e.g., facilities, human resources, security, to develop a program of plans and procedures to better prepare the organization and its employees for when, not if, a major emergency or disaster threatens the safety of your fellow employees and the organization's facilities.

This book, a tool to assist in strengthening your first line of defense, provides an overview of emergency management basics and a preparedness guide for all employees. Steps that front desk professionals can take before, during, and after an emergency or disaster strikes to be active participants in their organization's emergency management program are outlined. Specific procedures to follow in responding to a variety of safety and security threats are included. The human element of emergencies and disasters is also discussed. A listing of emergency management terms and acronyms, a readiness survey to assess your organization's current level of preparedness, emergency procedures in checklist format, a guide for conducting tabletop exercises, and a list of some important Web sites for future reference are found in the appendices.

One Size Does Not Fit All

The guidelines in this book, while written to reflect today's standards and best practices and guidance provided by government agencies, are, by necessity, to some extent generic. To be effective, an emergency preparedness and response program and its specific procedures must be tailored to meet the requirements and capabilities of your organization. Each organization is unique, and safety and security needs vary greatly from one organization to another. The size and layout of buildings and surrounding areas, the type of business or organization, even the organization's culture—all have to be considered. To be effective, emergency plans and procedures must take into account the disasters most likely to strike your location and must be based on the life safety and security systems that are in place, the organization's emergency response team structure and level of training, applicable regulatory requirements, and all local ordinances.

FRONT DESK
Security and Safety

SAFETY AND SECURITY BASICS

UNEXPECTED, negative events impact organizations of all types and can have devastating effects, and it is likely that your role in responding to these events is greater than ever before. Yet, few people have received formal emergency management education or training in how best to fulfill their responsibilities when there is a threat to safety and security. This chapter provides fundamental emergency management information. You may want to think of it as the Emergency Management 101 course you never had.

The Emergency Management Program

To better understand your front desk emergency response, safety, and security responsibilities, it is useful to review some emergency management basics and planning principles and standards.

An increasingly large number of organizations, from small companies to large international corporations and government agencies at all levels, have increased their efforts to provide a safe environment for everyone in their buildings, both on a day-to-day basis and when safety and security issues arise. While earlier emergency planning efforts tended to focus primarily on natural disasters, equal attention is now given to technological and incited (human-caused) disasters.

Current best practices call for more than emergency response *plans*. Equal in importance to the plan of action put into motion when emergencies occur are the steps taken before and after the emergency. Combined, the before, during, and after produce an ongoing comprehensive emergency management *program* that addresses all types of disasters through a dynamic process that includes four essential components: mitigation, preparedness, response, and recovery.

Mitigation is proactive steps taken before a disaster occurs with a goal of eliminating hazards to the greatest extent possible and lessening the impact of those threats that cannot be eliminated. While "mitigation" is the term of choice in the emergency management field, the word "prevention" is a reasonable synonym. The range of mitigation measures is broad. Mitigation may be as simple as enforcing good housekeeping to keep hallways clear from obstructions to avoiding overloaded electrical outlets to avoid fires, or securing computer monitors to desktops to prevent them from becoming flying objects during an earthquake. Mitigation may also be as complex as relocating technical equipment from the basement to an upper floor in areas subject to flooding, or installing a sophisticated, state-of-the art security system throughout the building.

Preparedness is the emergency management element typically given the most thought and attention. Preparedness includes organizing employee Emergency Response Teams, developing emergency plans and procedures, maintaining life safety systems and emergency supplies and equipment, and conducting emergency response training and evacuation drills.

Response to an emergency or disaster may begin while the event is still happening and may be of short duration. Actions during the response may include obtaining medical attention for injured or ill persons or evacuating and accounting for everyone in the building when the disaster occurs.

Recovery needs are based on the type and scope of the disaster. Recovery may be as simple as having everyone reenter the building and resume work following a short evacuation or as extreme as repairing or replacing structures and equipment in the wake of a severe disaster.

While an emergency management program provides for the protection of the organization's physical assets, its first and primary focus must be on protecting people.

Safety and Security in Your Organization

Become familiar with the life safety systems in your building. Life safety system requirements may be spelled out in local ordinances. They likely include automatic sprinkler systems; smoke detectors; battery- or generator-powered emergency lighting for exit signs, emergency stairwells, and limited floor lighting; fire alarm systems with fire alarm pulls and visible and audible alarms; and fire extinguishers. Most modern buildings have fire-rated emergency stairwells that are constructed to control the spread of smoke and fire, and exit doors that automatically unlock in an emergency. High-rise buildings are typically equipped with a fire panel that allows central monitoring of life safety systems by internal security staff and public safety officials who respond to emergencies.

Know what emergency supplies are maintained by your organization, where they are stored, and how to access them when needed. Most organizations' emergency preparations include stocking essential emergency supplies and equipment such as first-aid kits and basic tools. Some opt to stock a supply of food and water for employees and visitors in the event a disaster requires that they stay in the building for an extended time.

With heart disease being the leading cause of death in the United States, you may well find yourself responding to an employee or visitor experiencing a sudden cardiac arrest (SCA). Over the past several years an increasing number of organizations have made the decision to add automated external defibrillators (AEDs) to their emergency equipment. While cardiopulmonary resuscitation (CPR) buys the patient crucial time, it will not restart the heart. A defibrillator delivers an electric shock to the heart, allowing normal heartbeat to resume. Early defibrillation is the single most effective way to increase the odds of survival from SCA, and using a defibrillator immediately rather than waiting for paramedics to arrive can literally be life-saving. Anyone can use one with simple training. Defibrillators have visual and audible prompts that guide the user through the rescue process, and the machine won't shock if it detects a heartbeat.

A primary and key emergency response procedure is building evacuation. Evacuation drills may be required by local ordinances. It is critical that all employees receive training and that they practice evacuation procedures through a program of regularly scheduled drills to help ensure that everyone can safely and quickly evacuate the building. An evacuation route for each area of the building should be established and posted. Once out of the building, all employees should report to a pre-designated safe assembly area where a designated person, often a department manager or work group leader, accounts for employees to be certain that everyone made it out of the building safely. This last step is critical to a successful evacuation for two reasons. The first of these is to be certain that everyone made it out of the building without injury. The second, equally important reason is to avoid the possibility of sending emergency personnel into the building and into harm's way to look for someone who left the building but did not report to their assigned assembly area.

The Americans with Disabilities Act of 1990 (ADA) requires that employers provide reasonable accommodations to employees with special needs. Chief among these is to ensure that they can safely evacuate when necessary. If visitors are allowed on the work-site, your organization may want to invite voluntary disclosure about whether assistance is required in an emergency. For employees, contractors, and visitors who do self-identify a need for special assistance in an emergency due to a mobility, sight, hearing, or other special need, whether on a permanent or temporary basis, two employees may be assigned to provide assistance during a drill or when an actual building evacuation is ordered. This is referred to as the buddy system. A person with special needs knows the best way they can be assisted. By pre-designating the assistants ("buddies"), those with special needs and their assistants can talk about what is needed, and the "buddies" can receive any necessary training before a drill or actual evacuation. Contact local fire, police, and rescue units for direction about whether those with disabilities are to remain in their work area, assemble in a designated area, e.g., at the top of a fire stairway to wait for the arrival of rescue workers, or immediately evacuate. Providing emergency procedures in Braille, large print, text file, and cassette tape formats when needed is another important step.

Common security measures include on-site security guards, photo identification for all employees, and alarm systems. Metal detectors and closed circuit television (CCTV) may be used to monitor building entrances and exits and other areas requiring high-level security.

In very large organizations where all employees may not know one another, identification badges make it easy to know that a person passing you in the hallway belongs there.

The practice of having all visitors wear identification, usually an adhesive-backed paper ID tag, is a widely implemented security practice. This helps ensure that outsiders have gone through a security process, signed in, and have identified the person(s) they are visiting and the purpose for the visit. Having all visitors, known and unknown, sign in and out with the front desk provides a way of knowing who is on the premises. This is both a security procedure and also a way to track visitors who may need assistance if there is an emergency or if a building evacuation is necessary.

An emergency that directly impacts your organization may result in media interest in the actual incident, how your organization responded, and the final outcome. If so, news-paper, radio, and television reporters will be on-site to gather information. As providing information to the media appropriately is a learned skill, many organizations have a pol-icy that employees are not to give statements or interviews. This benefits both the organization and the employee. To avoid the possibility of being responsible for incomplete or incorrect information making its way to the front page of a newspaper or the evening news broadcast, all media requests for information should be referred to the Public Relations Department or other designated media representative whether or not a "no statement" policy has been adopted.

If your organization is not the sole tenant in the building, coordinating emergency plans and procedures with your co-tenant(s) is necessary for effective communication during an emergency and for a unified and integrated response by everyone in the building. This is particularly important when establishing building evacuation plans to avoid crowded emergency exits and stairwells and overlapping outdoor assembly areas.

Beyond the organization's safety and security measures, all employees must take ultimate responsibility for their own safety and security. Each employee should be familiar with the primary and alternate evacuation routes nearest their work space, know the location of the nearest fire alarm pull and know where to congregate and to whom to report after evacuating the building. Each and every employee, regardless of where they fit on the organization chart, should participate fully in each evacuation drill and attend employee safety and emergency training. If employee emergency response teams (ERTs) are in place, employees need to know who the ERT members are in their area of the building and know which employees, if any, are first-aid and CPR trained.

Emergency Response Teams

Emergency response teams (ERTs) staffed by employees are formed and trained to respond to emergencies and provide appropriate assistance to everyone in the building. ERTs coordinate with and augment internal security, other emergency professionals, and outside emergency agencies—fire, police, emergency medical technicians. ERTs, led by a coordinator, are typically composed of a floor warden, exit monitors, elevator monitors, searchers, and an assembly area coordinator for each floor or wing of the building. Team members receive training in their respective duties and, perhaps, first-aid, CPR, and blood-borne-pathogen training. Training in the use of fire extinguishers may be conducted for ERT members or for all employees.

ERT members are often equipped with hard hats and/or specially marked vests to make it easy to identify them. During an emergency response, the ERT has full authority over the response of all persons on the assigned floor. When an emergency occurs, everyone—employees and visitors—is to follow all directions given by ERT members, security staff, and any public safety officials who may be on site.

Home Preparedness

Preparing our homes and families for possible disasters is relatively simple, and also very easily postponed or ignored. While the first goal of home preparedness is to safeguard the people in your household, it also provides you with a measure of comfort when a widespread disaster impacts both your workplace and your home. You'll be better able to fulfill your disaster responsibilities at work knowing that you have taken steps to protect your home and family.

Home preparedness measures begin with making sure you have working smoke detectors. If they are battery-operated, replace the batteries at least twice annually. Use the dates for switching between standard time and daylight saving time as a reminder to change the batteries. Know the location of the shut-offs for water and gas and for the electrical service panel and how to turn off service.

Gather supplies for a home emergency kit. If the disaster is widespread, it may be three days, or even longer depending on the disaster type and severity, before local public safety and disaster relief organizations can provide assistance. Needed supplies can be divided into six basic categories: water and food, first-aid supplies including prescription- and non-prescription medications, tools, sanitation needs, and clothing. The rule-of-thumb requirement for water is one gallon per person per day for three days. The food supply should be sufficient to last for three days.

Specific examples of items to include with your home emergency supplies are a flashlight and battery-operated radio with extra batteries, extra eyeglasses, prescribed medications, a pocket knife, water purification tablets, first-aid handbook, three-day supply of food requiring no refrigeration, one gallon of water per person per day, plastic sheeting, paper and pencil, duct tape, heavy shoes or boots, work gloves, candles and waterproof matches, can opener, and sleeping bags or blankets. Including a few puzzles, games, and books is helpful should a disaster require staying at home, perhaps with no electric power, for longer periods of time. Additional special items may be required if there are infants, elderly individuals, or those needing special medical attention in the home.

A large garbage can or plastic storage bin can serve as good, inexpensive containers for your supplies. Duffle bags and backpacks are other options. Portability is important in the event of an evacuation. Store the disaster supplies in a convenient location, and make sure all household members know where it is located. At least annually inventory the supplies and replace items that have been used or whose expiration date has passed.

A detailed list of home emergency supplies and equipment can be obtained from local public safety officials, the Red Cross, or the Federal Emergency Management Agency (FEMA).

Keep originals or copies of critical documents in a safe deposit box. Some of the items you may want to include are driver's license, list of credit cards, checking and savings account numbers, insurance policies, passports, Social Security cards, immunization records, and wills.

Document your belongings and property. Prepare a household inventory, take date/time-stamped video or still pictures of each room in your home, photograph jewelry on a black cloth, gather originals or copies of certificates of authenticity for art objects and deeds to property, and proof of ownership documents (e.g., pink slips) for cars, boats, and other vehicles.

Identify evacuation routes, and agree upon a meeting place away from the home. To help household members reconnect in the event that a disaster prevents everyone from returning home, establish an out-of-area phone contact with a friend or family member. Conduct home drills to test your established plans and routes, both during daylight hours and at night with the lights off.

If there are school-aged children in the home, become familiar with their school's emergency response plans including the process used to release children following an emergency.

Develop a home disaster plan, gather your emergency supplies, and encourage your coworkers to do the same. Consider working with coworkers to institute a program to provide fellow employees with information about how to prepare their homes for disasters. Some organizations go the extra mile and hold an annual emergency preparedness event for all employees. Disaster preparedness information is handed out, local emergency officials are on hand, and emergency supplies and equipment are available for purchase.

How Prepared Are You?

The Readiness Assessment (Appendix 2) is a tool to help you measure how prepared your organization and your front desk are to respond to safety and security threats. The results provide a "snapshot" of your organization's safety and security culture and the front desk's level of readiness. While the total score will provide you with a simple measurement of your organization's preparedness, the assessment's greatest value will come from using it to identify areas that can be improved and enhanced to increase the organization's capabilities and better prepare the front desk to act in response to future emergencies and disasters.

FRONT DESK ROLES AND RESPONSIBILITIES

ESSENTIALLY, safety and security efforts are as much a state of mind as they are the use of security systems and countermeasures. While written policies, procedures, and plans and equipment are essential to effective safety and security and emergency management programs, without the active participation of all employees, the best of programs will fail. This is true of no one more than the organization's front desk staff.

Having a complete understanding of your organization's safety, security, and emergency management programs is vital to enable you to fulfill your responsibilities. As a way of determining if you have good, basic knowledge of how the organization approaches these programs, ask yourself the following questions.

❑ Do we have safety, security, and emergency management programs?

❑ Is there one program that covers everything, or are there separate programs for emergency management and safety and security?

❑ Who has the responsibility for maintaining and updating these programs and the related procedures?

❑ If we have multiple locations, are procedures the same at all locations?

❑ What printed emergency procedures have been provided to all employees?

❏   Are these procedures part of the orientation for all new employees?

❏   Do all employees receive refresher training in emergency procedures?

❏   What reports am I to make following an emergency or a security breach, and to whom do I make the reports?

If you are not sure about the answers to any of these questions, seek out the people who do have the information and ask them to fill in any blanks for you. Some things you do each day are fundamental to the continued safety and security of your organization, your fellow employees, and visitors to your building. Often taken for granted, these standard procedures are the foundation of your organization's safety and security.

In addition to organization-wide, day-to-day safety and security procedures, the front desk needs to be involved in all elements of the organization's emergency management program: mitigation, preparedness, emergency responsibilities, and post-emergency responsibilities.

Day-to-Day

I was recently in a company's elegant modern main entry. The well-appointed lobby with decorator chairs and sofas, beautiful artwork, and plush carpeting was equipped with state-of-the-art life safety system components including smoke detectors, sprinklers, and copies of evacuation procedures and routes on one of the glass-topped tables. The area was equipped with well-placed security cameras and signage indicating that all visitors are to check in and sign the visitors' log. I knew that the front desk was also equipped with a panic button that could be used to alert security and an additional button that would automatically lock the entrance doors. Great—until I walked in the front door and passed the receptionist, who finally looked up from reading a magazine and said "hello" as I walked into the main section of the building.

What's wrong with this picture? The receptionist did not know me. Who was I? Where was I going once I entered the main part of the building? Quite simply, the person at the front desk failed to do her job by following basic established procedures. Avoid falling into the, "Nothing has ever happened here, and I don't think it ever will" trap. Don't allow a failure to regularly follow all procedures "just this one time" to become your organization's vulnerability.

First and foremost, keep an eye on what's happening in the front desk area. Avoid sitting with your head down reading a book. Don't get involved in lengthy conversations with colleagues or lengthy personal phone conversations. Be aware of who and what is coming through the door. If someone sitting in the waiting area moves, be aware of where they are going.

If employee badges are required at your location, do everything you can to maintain 100 percent compliance. If a colleague, even one you know well, is not wearing their badge or if the badge is not visible, remind them of the requirements. If there is a metal detector, have everyone go through it. No by-passers allowed!

While it might be easier to just ignore some of these standard procedures—after all it's your coffee buddy Sue or Joe or maybe a company executive—there are policies and requirements and it's your job to enforce them. No exceptions. Consider this case in point for following all security guidelines to the letter at all times.

The headquarters office of an international law firm began experiencing thefts. Items including smaller pieces of equipment, supplies, and employees' portable CD players and wallets began disappearing on a fairly regular basis. Security conducted an investigation, first suspecting that an employee or perhaps cleaning company employees might be responsible. After calling in security specialists who placed an undercover person in the office, the culprit was found to be both obvious and unbelievable.

Law firms are notorious for working long hours when attorneys and the staff are preparing court documents or getting ready for a hearing or trial, often eating meals in the office to continue their work. People at this law firm had a favorite pizza parlor that they regularly called to have their meals delivered, and there was one delivery person, we'll call him Bob, who was everyone's favorite. He often had a funny story to share and knew many employees by name. Known well by the front desk staff, Bob was allowed to circumvent front desk security procedures and come and go at will. Got it yet?

Good old Bob would walk into the building carrying the food in an insulated container to keep it warm. He would then leave with the insulated container filled with items he was able to pick up as he made his way through the office–a portable radio here, a cell phone there. No one ever questioned him or thought to look in the container he was carrying. Making an exception for Bob the pizza delivery guy proved very expensive for the firm and its employees, as well as an embarrassment to all, particularly the front desk staff.

If you have keys or an access card to the building or interior doors, keep them safe. Don't lend your keys to anyone or let anyone use a key or access card with which you have been entrusted. Don't leave your keys, access card, or ID card on a desk or counter-top in your work area. It's best to always keep keys on your person or in a locked cabinet or drawer. Hiding places that you consider secret often don't remain secret for long. If your key, access card, or ID card is lost or stolen, report it to security, or others as designated, immediately. Don't label keys with a room number. If petty cash is kept at the front desk, always keep it out of sight and locked away.

If you must leave your work area for any reason, even "just for a minute or two," lock everything. Don't leave a purse, briefcase, or bag at an unattended front desk.

If you're working on a computer, clear the screen and log off before walking away. Always follow all internet/intranet security guidelines; even one exception can create a breach in computer security that may be widespread and costly. Do not leave your computer password where someone might see it or easily find it. Again, there are no "perfect" hiding places.

If you have work papers on the desktop, put them in a drawer. Avoid leaving documents in shared printers or facsimile machines in public areas. If you work with printed material that is in any way confidential or proprietary, do not simply throw it in a wastebasket in the front desk area. If there is not one in place now, request a shredder for the front desk area. If that is not possible, dispose of discarded papers in an area of the building not accessible to outsiders.

Avoid discussing confidential information or organization business in front of visitors, and remind your fellow employees to follow suit. Remember that even a seemingly insignificant conversation may include content that should not be heard outside the organization. Information that seems inconsequential to you may be of great interest to competitors or other outsiders or even to employees who may use it to the detriment of the organization or employees. Your organization's business plans, customer information, and other sensitive data are an asset to be protected.

If possible, stagger the times you take breaks and leave the area to go to lunch. Don't be too predictable. Make it a point to brief the person relieving you. Who is in the waiting area and who they are waiting to see? Are any deliveries or service persons expected? Has anything happened that is out of the ordinary? Let your relief know what is happening and get answers to these same questions when you return.

Always be aware of your surroundings. Report any suspicious activity such as an unfamiliar person remaining in the front desk area for no apparent reason or someone who returns to the building multiple times in a short amount of time for no reason. Immediately report the presence of unauthorized building occupants, such as terminated employees, or outsiders who have been identified as being safety or security risks. If you have a no-solicitors policy, make sure it is enforced.

Always follow all access controls to the letter—no exceptions. Screen all visitors to verify that they have a legitimate need to be in the building and that they are expected. Have everyone sign in and issue them a temporary identification badge. Never assume that someone has a right to be in the building. Check the identity of unknown persons.

Recently, in the reception area of an international corporation I noticed a large sphere-shaped "sculpture" approximately four feet in diameter on a corner of the reception counter. On closer inspection, I realized that what I first thought was a piece of art-work was actually created with used adhesive-backed visitor badges stuck together to form a large ball. The result was a great place for departing visitors to deposit their badges and an interesting lobby conversation piece. The fact that all visitors see that using the badges is a standard practice is a more subtle benefit of displaying this very special "creation."

All visitors should be escorted while in the private areas of the building. Each visitor should be announced to the person they wish to see by phone or intercom and then be asked to wait in the front desk area for the employee who will escort them. Following their visit the person should be escorted back to the front desk to sign out. An enforced policy that requires all visitors to be escorted while in the building is both a good security practice and old-fashioned good manners.

I've witnessed many organizations that have the sign-in procedure down pat only to frequently ignore the sign-out step. Both steps are equally important to be able to get a true picture of who is in the building at any given time.

I recall my first visit to a high-tech company where, after indicating the name of the person I was there to see, I was directed by the receptionist, who had never seen me before and who asked for no identification, to "Go through those doors, down the corridor to the left, pass the research and development department, turn right, pass the human resources department, and continue down the hall until you get to Sam's office. I think he's in this afternoon." As she turned me loose in the building, I thought what a good thing it was that I wasn't a competitor interested in the new products being developed by this company that was operating in a highly-competitive market or that I wasn't a disgruntled former employee with a grudge against someone in HR.

Some organizations are adding a requirement to check visitors' identification when they enter the building; in a more limited number of locations, two pieces of identification are requested. Other more stringent requirements may include searching packages, purses, and briefcases taken into the building. Whether to add these additional check-in procedures is a decision that must be made by management based on experience and the level of security needed.

If you see someone begin to leave the front desk area and head for other parts of the building without checking in, ask, "Can I help you," or "Can I let someone know you are here?" Do not give them access and do not leave them unescorted. If the person is someone who should not be there, they may likely ignore you or may give you a curt answer and head for an exit, stairway, or elevator. Do not try to stop them. Call security or 9-1-1 immediately and provide a description of the person.

For example, imagine that near the end of the business day you see a man unknown to you enter the lobby and sits down in the waiting area. Upon asking how you can be of help, the barely audible response is that he is checking his appointment book for the name of the person he is to see. A few minutes later as you are answering a phone call, you look up to see the man heading toward the door to the main part of the building. Without acknowledging your request that he check in at the desk, the man picks up his pace and with an angry look on his face, continues into the building.

Without hesitation, call security or 9-1-1. There is an unknown person in the building. You do not know who he is there to see, exactly where in the building he is headed, or his purpose for being there. Stay at the front desk to be available to give a description of the person.

If someone is loitering or acting suspiciously in or near the front desk area and you have any hesitancy about approaching them, call security or another pre-identified source of assistance. Report the person's location and description. If possible to do so discreetly, keep an eye on the person until help arrives.

Any time you see a person committing an illegal act or criminal offense, don't hesitate. Call 9-1-1 immediately and inform security and/or others as identified in your organization's security procedures. While the details of the incident are still fresh in your mind, write down a description of those involved, exactly what happened, and the time and location of the offense. If the person(s) have left the area, report where they were last seen and their exit route. If your organization does not have an incident report form, you may want to create one to provide an outline of information to be noted.

Some front desks are also a central receiving point for packages. Even in organizations where most deliveries go through a central receiving area or a mail center, it is not uncommon for an occasional package or envelope to make its way to the front desk.

If deliveries are regularly received by the front desk, validate vendor lists of all routine deliveries and repair services. Take notice and report any suspicious packages. Even a briefcase that has been left unattended and for which you can not readily identify an owner should be considered suspect. Do not handle or attempt to move any questionable item. It's important to keep track of what comes in the building. . .and what goes out.

Do not allow anyone—employee or visitor—to remove computers, peripherals, or other equipment from the building unless you know who they are and that they have permission to do so. In today's highly computerized world, while the equipment leaving the building does have financial value, it may also contain confidential or proprietary information that the organization can ill afford to let walk out the door. Some organizations have established a policy and system for tracking equipment taken home by employees. A form is signed by a manager giving permission for the item(s) to be taken from the building. These forms are tracked by the front desk, and items not checked back in within the specified time are reported to the manager who signed the permission form for follow-up.

Another security procedure being used by more organizations today than ever before, particularly where data security is highly critical, is to have all visitors check in their laptop computers at the front desk. The computer's serial number is recorded and then cross-checked when the visitor leaves the building with the computer. This ensures that the same computers that enter the building leave the building and that no exchanges are made.

There may be a question about the necessity of these systems, seen as extreme by some. Based on the needed level of security, each organization must make a determination as to whether to adopt a policy requiring more stringent procedures to track articles passing the front desk. An incident that occurred at a large corporation a few years ago may present a good case for establishing these or similar policies and procedures at your location.

An employee discovered that an external computer hard drive was missing. While not being able to account for any equipment is always a nuisance, this missing hard drive caused great alarm and extreme concern as it contained the names, addresses, and bank account numbers of retired employees. The company took immediate steps first to rectify the situation by contacting all those whose information was contained on the hard drive and then to institute strict procedures for employees and others leaving the building with any property belonging to the company. And for those wondering, the mystery was never solved, and the hard drive is still missing. We'll never know if the hard drive was discarded by mistake, if it was taken by someone who intended to use the information on the drive for illegal purposes, or if it was just a case of someone wanting a hard drive for their home computer system.

Some safety and security procedures require you to say "No" or involve you in making certain that a person who would rather not do so follow established guidelines. When that happens, a few simple steps can make it easier for you.

It's Okay to Say No

Good front desk professionals are polite, gracious, and often go the extra mile to accommodate everyone with whom they come in contact. While your comfort level in doing so is likely not always great, there are times when saying "No," is absolutely necessary for the safety and security of the organization and its employees.

You can't accept a package without the authorization of the person to whom it is addressed. You can't allow an unknown outsider to take pictures of the lobby. You can't permit a friendly, seemingly nonthreatening person to go into the building without proper identification. You can't let a fellow employee bring friends or family members into the building without appropriate clearance. These are situations when saying "No" may be quite uncomfortable but is the necessary and right thing to do. Here are some tips that may make not saying "Yes," a little easier.

First remember and mentally tell yourself that saying "No" is the appropriate response. If the organization's policies and procedures are that is the answer you are to give is "No" then it is appropriate and right for you to do so.

Consider this example: A woman with a notepad and pen in hand approaches you and asks you about a recent downsizing at your organization. She wants your opinion about how the layoffs were handled, whether you thought they were necessary, and the names of a few of the people who lost their jobs. It quickly becomes apparent to you that the woman is a reporter. In a comeback to your initial response that the organization's policy is that employees not give media interviews, she aggressively reels off a list of reasons why you should give her the information. I only need you to give me a short statement. Don't you want to get the employees' side of this story out there? The organization doesn't have anything to hide, does it? Just give me a little insight on what's going on. You can trust me; I won't repeat anything you tell me.

Remember that you don't have to respond immediately, take a few seconds to organize your thoughts. You know what the policy is and you are in charge.

Always maintain a professional image and avoid being argumentative or confrontational. Check to make sure you are not conveying a nonassertive image by keeping your eyes downcast and avoiding eye contact, having poor posture, fidgeting or shifting your body. You also don't want to exhibit an aggressive attitude or stance.

It is often easier to be assertive by starting your response with the word "No." "No, I cannot allow you to go immediately to Mr. Smith's office. No unescorted guests are permitted beyond the main lobby." This makes your response clear to the visitor and helps you remain committed to your response.

Don't qualify or hedge your statements. "I think that you aren't supposed to take that laptop home without your manager's approval" makes it seem that you are not quite sure about what you are to do or that there's room for negotiation. A simple "The requirement is that all employees have written permission to take equipment from the property" leaves no doubt.

Sound confident and secure in your statements. Ending a statement by tagging on a question—either by asking an actual question or by an upward voice inflection—indicates insecurity and a lack of confidence. Avoid "Take a seat in the waiting area while I check to see if you are expected, okay?" Erase the okay that changes your assertive statement to a question and opens the door for discussion.

Using certain phrases destroys the authority of what you are saying. "You're not going to like having to take the extra time, but we require all parcels to be delivered to the loading dock." Don't preface your statements with comments that diminish their impact or importance. "We require that all parcels be delivered to the loading dock," is the message and all you need to say.

When saying "No," use assertive nonverbal skills. Keep your voice firm, clear, and direct. Avoid speaking too quickly. Pay attention to what the other person is saying. Letting them know you are listening to them does not indicate that you agree or that you will give in to their request.

Here's an example: A customer is at the front desk, demanding to see the manager of customer service immediately about a billing adjustment. You know that policy requires that all requests for adjustments must be made in writing. First, remain calm and diffuse the situation by saying "Tell me about what has happened, and then I'll see how we can help you." While she tells you about her situation, occasionally nod or say, "Go on," or "I see," to let her know you are listening. While it will still be necessary to deny the woman's request to see the customer service manager, just having someone listen will give her a chance to calm down. You can then say no to her original demand and provide an alternative way for solving her problem.

If it helps you to take a more assertive approach, stand up. Whether sitting or standing, square up your shoulders and look the person in the eye. Simultaneously shake your head and say, "No." When standing, keep your arms relaxed at your sides, your feet slightly apart and your knees slightly flexed. You'll look as though you're ready to move and take action. When sitting, keep your head up and keep your hands above the counter or desk.

If there are times when you're not sure that "No" is the best response or if you are being repeatedly cajoled or coaxed to change your response, take a breath and take the time to think it over. Remind yourself that the decision is entirely up to you. You are in charge of the front desk. You know what you need to do; don't be forced into a decision you will later regret.

Remember that if you do say "Yes" when you need to say "No," you may endanger the safety and security of your organization and fellow employees.

Dealing with Angry People

There may be times when a visitor to your building will become angry when hearing "No," or when an angry or hostile customer or client confronts you about a problem. Dealing appropriately with these individuals may head off a potential emergency or disaster.

Dealing with unhappy, sarcastic, angry, or abusive people at the front desk is stressful and can take a great deal of your time. While we need to accept that people will get angry at times, such people are a challenge to deal with at best. In more extreme cases they may even swear at you, attempt to intimidate you, or make threats. Most of these situations are easily handled, and while every hostile situation is different and must be dealt with on a case-by-case basis, there are some suggestions that will help keep a bad situation from escalating into disastrous situation.

For example, you see a man walk through the door and stride quickly toward the front desk. He is tight-lipped, red-faced, and has a tense body posture. Glaring at you, in a very agitated tone, his first words are, "I have left several phone messages for John Gray over the past two weeks, and he has not returned my phone calls. I have to see him, and if he doesn't see me now, there's going to be real trouble." He slams his fist down on the desk. What do you do?

❏ First, be aware of the signs that indicate that a person approaching the front desk may be irritated or upset. Even before they speak, angry and hostile people often telegraph their mood with nonverbal messages. Watch for hunched shoulders, clenched fists, an angry expression, or perhaps a red face, or heavy, stomping footsteps. Restlessness and either staring you down or avoiding eye contact are other indications that the person approaching will require some special attention.

❏ If you believe an approaching person may be angry, prepare yourself. Take a deep breath and remind yourself that you are absolutely capable of handling the situation.

❏ Let the approaching person see a calm, friendly yet businesslike person. Don't react too quickly; take things slowly. Avoid becoming angry yourself. Responding in kind to shouting or trading insults will only exacerbate a bad situation and might result in negative consequences for you. Remember that the person is not angry with you personally. While you are the first person with whom they have contact, their issue is likely with the organization in general, a situation, a product or service, or perhaps another individual in the organization.

❏ Speak in a friendly manner and greet the person cordially, by name if possible. Show your interest and concern. Listen carefully to what the person is saying before beginning your response. In the majority of cases, while they do want the problem fixed or the situation changed, an angry person does not necessarily expect you personally to do so. They want to be heard. Empathize, perhaps with a phrase like, "Most people would be angry if their bill was incorrect three months in a row." Remember that an angry person doesn't really hear anything that you say and is not ready to solve the problem. Keep listening; focus on acknowledging the person's feelings. Only after they start to calm down after having vented their anger and having made clear to you how upset they are is it possible to move toward finding a solution to the problem.

❏ Monitor the situation and the person's actions. If your attempts to calm the individual are unsuccessful and if you have any reason to believe that the situation is worsening or that your own safety and that of others in the area is in any way in jeopardy, do not deal with an escalated situation. Remember that you are not obligated to tolerate foul language or abusive behavior. If your threshold of tolerance for abusive behavior is crossed or if threats are made, take the steps necessary to deal with the situation. Contact security. Use the panic button. Signal someone to call 9-1-1. Do whatever the specific situation requires to ensure everyone's safety.

❑ When the angry person is on the phone rather than standing in front of you, follow the same general guidelines. As with an angry person standing at the front desk, take any threats the caller makes seriously and take the appropriate actions immediately.

Front Desk Mitigation

Mitigation in the front desk area may require that you be proactive and take the lead. For the safety of visitors and employees, check to be certain your front desk area does not present any safety risks. Work with facilities or engineering to check for and correct any safety risks. For example, are rugs and floor mats in good condition? Is there a possibility that frayed rugs or mats or a slippery floor could cause falls?

Coordinate with facilities and security to make the front desk area as easy to monitor as possible. If feasible, in a front desk area that has more than one entrance, designate only one door to be used by everyone for entrance and exit. This makes it easier to observe who is coming into and leaving the building. Doors not intended for ingress and egress should not be propped open to allow people to enter unseen. Are entrances kept clear of obstructions at all times?

Position the front desk to make it as easy as possible to see all those coming and going and to provide the best possible view of doorways and of persons who have not yet signed in. This may include moving large plants and rearranging furniture in the guest waiting area. A flat surface at a suitable height for visitor sign-in is a plus. If you do data entry at the front desk, position the computer monitor to allow you to simultaneously use the computer and keep an eye on the front desk area.

Consider adding entry or lobby signage that directs all visitors to sign in at the front desk or, if it is part of your security procedures, an advisory that all packages, handbags, and briefcases carried in by visitors are subject to being searched.

Silent duress alarm switches, often referred to as "panic buttons," are an invaluable security tool at reception points. A simple touch triggers these hidden buttons, summoning assistance without overt actions. Increasingly common tools at front desks, panic buttons are also used in the offices of executives and their assistants and other high-security areas. If a panic alarm is not in place, check the feasibility of having one installed. Work with security experts to choose a location for the alarm; it needs to be easy to activate without drawing attention.

The ability to lock the main entrance door remotely from the front desk is another step that may be considered. This is particularly advisable in areas where public demonstrations are a frequent occurrence or in generally unsafe locations.

Working with security, facilities, and, as appropriate, others in your organization, establish code words that can be used to quickly request assistance. Delivered by phone or in person, these code words summon immediate help without letting others know that the request is being made.

In some organizations the front desk area is removed from the rest of the building or in a somewhat remote area. If that true for your work area, a good security procedure is to establish set times during the day when you will check in with a specific person, perhaps in security or facilities. If the designated person doesn't hear from you, for example, when you first arrive at work, at 9:10, 11:15, 1:20, 3:25, and again just before your leave the building, they will phone you or come to the front desk to make sure there are no problems.

Preparedness Responsibilities

As with most things in life, when you must take action to respond to a safety or security threat, the better prepared you are, the more effective the outcome will be.

Depending on the size of the organization, you may be asked to be a member of the emergency response team for your area of the building, or your role may be to manage the emergency response in the area of the front desk. In either case, it is important that you know what actions you are expected to take, that you be familiar with the role and responsibilities of the ERT, and that you understand how you are to collaborate and coordinate with the ERT organization.

Know which employees have been trained and certified in CPR and first aid, their work locations, and their extension numbers. Update this list no less often than twice annually to add newly trained employees, delete those whose certifications may have expired, and correct for changes in work locations or extension numbers.

While the first telephone number to call for any type of emergency or disaster is 9-1-1 to contact the fire department, local police or sheriff's office, and paramedics, there are other numbers that you should have at your fingertips. Include the internal numbers for security, the emergency response team coordinator, and facilities. An ambulance service, the nearest hospital or urgent care facility, your alarm company, the local postal inspector, and local FBI officials are some of the other numbers you may want to add to your list.

While it's a good practice to have these numbers programmed in your automatic dialer, in some major emergencies and disasters, the phone system may not work. Automatic dialers not equipped with battery backup will not function when the emergency results in a power outage. Having a printed list available is essential. Print the emergency contact list using a large, readable font. Consider using colored paper—yellow, orange, or lime green—and laminating the list. Keep it where it is always visible, and be certain everyone who staffs the front desk knows exactly where it is located. Check all numbers for accuracy at least quarterly and make any necessary changes or corrections.

Keep a flashlight and two sets of extra batteries at your work area. In the event of a power outage, it will help you carry out your emergency responsibilities and can also be used to help reassure and guide visitors.

A small portable radio often comes in handy to monitor weather conditions in natural disasters or to listen to news reports for updates on other disasters. If you are in an area that frequently experiences severe weather, e.g., hurricanes, tornadoes, severe winter storms, a National Oceanic and Atmospheric Administration (NOAA) weather radio with a tone alert feature that signals when severe weather is approaching and provides information about what to do is particularly helpful. Again, keep two extra sets of replacement batteries. Replace both the flashlight and radio batteries every six months or when their expiration date nears to ensure that they will work when needed.

Review all emergency plans at least once a quarter. If you note areas needing updating or a need for additional procedures, talk with the person in the organization who is responsible for maintaining the plan.

Be familiar with the layout of the front desk area and the surrounding areas. Know the location of the nearest fire alarms, fire extinguishers, first-aid supplies, and emergency equipment. Know the location of the emergency exits, evacuation routes, and designated outdoor assembly areas. Walk through the evacuation route for your area once a month. Check monthly to see if there have been any changes in the emergency response team members on your floor or the first-aid- and CPR-trained employees nearest the front desk. These individuals may change frequently as people are reassigned or leave the organization.

Attend any offered safety and security training. If you feel that you need additional training, check to see if it can be made available to you. Participate in all evacuation drills and emergency exercises.

As an additional preparedness measure, some organizations provide visitors with a one-page list of basic emergency instructions that includes an evacuation map for the floor they will be visiting. Discuss with those in charge of your emergency management program whether this may be a good option.

Making the necessary preparations now will enable you to act quickly and efficiently when an emergency or disaster happens.

Emergency Responsibilities

Your responsibilities in an emergency response will depend on your organization's emergency management program and related safety and security plans and procedures.

Whatever your role, here are some basic guidelines.

One rule to remember above all others: protect life, including your own. Never put your own well-being in jeopardy. If you are injured, you will not only need assistance, but will be unable to help others.

Stay calm. Breathe deeply and slowly to help control your stress. Remember visitors and fellow employees will look to you for reassurance. Stay focused on what needs to be done now. Be decisive. Take control of the front desk area and provide clear, concise instructions in accordance with established procedures. Remember that visitors are not familiar with your building or procedures; they will rely on you. Make sure they understand what they are to do and how they are to exit the building. If necessary, personally guide them out of the building and to the assembly area.

A long-standing principle in first aid is to do no harm. Never attempt to provide assistance that is beyond your capabilities or for which you are untrained. Remember that you can't be all things to all people. Each person has ultimate responsibility for their own safety.

When you are in doubt, always err on the side of caution. If you are not certain whether you need to call 9-1-1 or security, don't hesitate. Make the call. Wait for emergency personnel to arrive. If the professionals require your help, they will let you know what is needed.

Follow established plans and procedures to the extent possible. In cases when, because of unusual or unforeseen circumstances, doing so will not be safe, or in situations when established procedures, for whatever reason, will just not work, be flexible and creative. First, assess the situation, and then act to best address the situation.

Based on factors including the location of the front desk area, building configuration, and staffing, you may be assigned to an ERT. Whether or not you are a member of the ERT organization, it is important to understand how the teams are organized and the roles of the team members. While the composition of teams and specific roles and responsibilities may vary somewhat, most are similar to the organization chart in Figure 1.

As required by the specific emergency situation, the ERT members direct and coordinate response by individual employees, conduct basic search and rescue, and assist in accounting for building occupants following an evacuation. They provide first aid or make the notifications necessary to get medical help for ill or injured persons. They calm and reassure people to help prevent panic. Often just knowing that there are trained teams responding to the situation allays fears and provides reassurance.

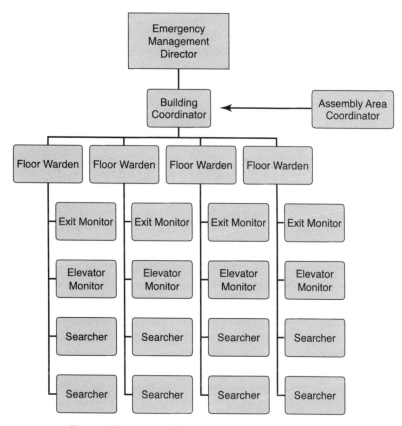

Figure 1. Emergency Response Team (ERT) Organization.

One of the benefits of ERT members wearing identifying vests and perhaps hard hats is that it lets people see that there is an organized and trained team taking charge of the emergency situation. Some organizations take the additional step of identifying ERT members and their normal work locations with special signage to provide another way to reassure employees and visitors that there are people who will assist them when an emergency occurs.

The emergency management director has responsibility for managing and coordinating the organization's entire emergency management program. Specific duties typically include organizing ERTs, procuring supplies and equipment, arranging for appropriate training for ERT members and the general employee population, and coordinating with security and other departments as necessary.

The building ERT coordinator directs the ERT members and reports to the emergency management director. The building ERT coordinator has full, life-safety-related decision-making authority for their facility during emergencies. The building ERT coordinator may also have responsibility for coordinating with security, facilities, and any outside agencies involved in responding to the emergency. In organizations with multiple buildings, a building ERT coordinator is appointment for each building.

The floor warden oversees the emergency preparedness and response program on the assigned floor. When an emergency occurs, the floor warden is typically responsible for directing the other ERT members on the assigned floor, employee and visitor response, compiling status information from other team members on the assigned floor, and reporting to the building ERT coordinator. Additional floor warden responsibilities may include conducting preliminary damage surveys and providing status reports to the building ERT coordinator once the initial response is concluded.

Coordinating with the floor warden, exit monitors direct employees and guests toward the emergency exit while helping to keep everyone calm and providing assistance as needed.

On upper floors, elevators monitors direct everyone away from the elevators and toward the emergency exits, again keeping people calm and aiding anyone needing assistance. Both exit monitors and elevator monitors remind employees to report to their assigned assembly after existing the building.

Searchers, always working in pairs, ensure that the assigned area has been vacated in the event of evacuation. They conduct a systematic search of the assigned area, including restrooms, file rooms, lunch and coffee rooms, conference rooms, and storage areas to ensure that everyone in their assigned area heard the alarm and has completely vacated once an evacuation is ordered. Searchers close all doors as each room and area is checked.

The assembly area coordinator is typically responsible for reporting to the designated outdoor assembly area following a building evacuation and directing all employees to congregate by department, work group, or building area as pre-designated. Once employees have gathered, the assembly area coordinator collects reports from all floor wardens and confers with work supervisors and coworkers to see whether everyone has made it to the assembly area; he or she then provides a complete status report to the building coordinator that includes a list of those unaccounted for and their last known location.

A discussion of ERTs always reminds me again of the importance of tailoring every aspect of an emergency management program, not only to meet the organization's requirements and capabilities, but also to fit with the organization's culture.

As a case in point, at one company it was even necessary to change an ERT position title to mesh better with the company's culture. In introducing the ERT organization structure to the employees of the company, where the average employee age at the time was approximately twenty-six, there was immediate and extreme dissatisfaction with the term "floor warden." Many employees viewed the title "warden" as one that belonged in a penal institution, not in their company. To maintain a satisfactory comfort level for everyone, the floor warden became the floor coordinator. Was this an insignificant, unnecessary change?

While the initial response may be a resounding, "Absolutely," the importance of integrating emergency management into the organization's culture cannot be overstated. It is the organization's culture that dictates employee behavior and ultimately has much to do with the extent to which all employees support (or fail to support) the emergency management program and ERT members. Something as small as changing a position title may have great long-range value to the success of the emergency management program.

All employees need to fully understand that during an emergency the ERT has full authority over the response by occupants on the assigned floor or area regardless of team members' day-to-day position or responsibilities. Everyone is to follow all directions given by ERT members, building safety and security staff, or public safety officials.

It is important to make sure the emergency management program includes all employees. I have seen examples of organizations that have an excellent ERT program for employees who work the standard 8:00 to 5:00, Monday through Friday schedule and yet forget that not all employees work that same schedule. If your organization has shift workers, don't forget those who work evenings, nights, and weekends. Other organizations, where there are not shift workers, may have employees who often work other than the normal hours of operation, staying late into the evening or coming in on weekends. ERTs need to be organized for all shifts. Emergency training must be provided across all shifts, and appropriate plans and procedures should be developed for employees working after formal work hours have ended.

Another possible scenario for you is that that the duties of some of the ERT members will be collapsed and the person staffing the front desk will fulfill multiple ERT duties for that area, typically those of the exit monitor, elevator monitor, and searchers. If that is the case, you will be responsible for directing employees and visitors in the front desk area along the designated evacuation route to the emergency exit, and away from any elevators in the front desk area, and advising everyone of where they are to assemble once they are outside the building. Before you leave, conduct a sweep of the front desk area, and, after ensuring that all employees and visitors have vacated the area, close, but do not lock, all doors.

Once outside the building, report to your designated assembly area and, to the extent possible, account for everyone who was in the front desk area at the time the evacuation was ordered. Follow all established reporting channels. If you are not able to account for everyone who was in the front desk area, immediately tell the assembly area coordinator or other appropriate person(s) who is missing and where you last saw them. Request first aid or medical attention for anyone who may have been injured during the evacuation, and continue to calm and reassure people who may be upset.

If there are reporters on the scene, do not make comments or give interviews and discourage others from doing so.

Once the danger has passed, there is still work to be done. Comprehensive emergency plans include actions to be taken after the emergency or disaster has ended.

Post-Emergency Responsibilities

Check to see what is expected of you post-emergency, once people are safe or have received medical attention and public safety officials who may have responded have left.

If a formal debrief is conducted, attend and give your assessment of how well the response was handled. In place of, or in addition to, the debrief, you may be asked to provide a written report either by completing a standard report form or by writing a narrative of your perspective of what occurred. Even if you are not asked to do so, write a report and send it to those in the organization who oversee emergency programs. Include in your report both what worked well during the response and what needs to be improved. Based on your evaluation, include a list of additional equipment that is needed, any procedures that are missing or that do not provide sufficient details, or the need for better training for designated response team members or all employees.

To the extent possible, move forward with making the corrective actions that you have identified as being necessary. If you can't personally make the changes, follow up with those who can to avoid having the same items become problems again when the next emergency or disaster occurs.

Good emergency management requires a team effort. You can't do it alone.

Your Support System

You have many allies, both in your organization and in the community, to assist you in preparing for and carrying out your safety and security responsibilities.

Establish and maintain open lines of communication with others in your organization who play a role in protecting the safety and security of employee and visitors. These channels of communication are of significant help not just when an emergency happens, but in the mitigation and preparedness processes as well.

If your organization has a safety coordinator or an emergency management coordinator, meet with them to learn exactly what programs are in place, what your role and responsibilities are, and what support is available to you.

The security director and the on-site security staff have likely identified the risks that are the greatest threat to the organization in general, as well as those that are specific to the front desk. They will provide you with guidance on what to do in the event of a security threat or breach. Coordinate with them when emergencies occur. Call them if extra help is needed, or if you are just not comfortable handling a situation on your own.

The human resources management department (HR) or personnel department is your best source of detailed information about your organization's policies on violence in the workplace. They can also help you obtain needed safety and security training. If HR has oversight of Occupational Safety and Health Administration (OSHA) compliance, they may take ownership of conducting a facility risk survey, occupational health and safety issues, and placement of needed safety equipment. HR can take the lead in developing a communications plan to disseminate correct, rumor-free information to employees to prevent panic immediately after an emergency and to provide appropriate updates in the days or weeks following a disaster. If your organization has an employee assistance program managed by HR, that program is the natural link to an excellent source of post-trauma stress counseling following an emergency.

The facilities or engineering department can help facilitate mitigation measures such as repairing nonfunctioning exit signs or rearranging the front desk area.

Check around. These are just some of the internal resources you have to assist you. There are likely others. Outside the organization there are also many sources of valuable information and assistance that are prepared to help you and your organization.

Public safety officials are the professionals who will respond and take charge when an emergency occurs. The two primary local agencies providing assistance are fire and law enforcement. In addition to responding to emergencies, these agencies are experts and are a great source of information and guidance in emergency preparedness planning. Available services vary from one jurisdiction to another, and there is seldom a charge for any assistance provided. In some instances fire authorities will initiate contact with your organization as part of their code enforcement and fire prevention program.

Both the fire departments and law enforcement agencies will review your safety and security procedures and emergency response plans and provide feedback for improvements. They may also review the related employee training curriculum.

The local fire authority can provide information on the possible threats and hazards in your area. They will check to ensure that your life safety systems and emergency procedures meet local codes and ordinances and make suggestions to bring your organization into compliance. They will review your evacuation plan and offer guidance on mapping the best exit routes from your building. Representatives from the fire department can help you plan an evacuation drill, observe the drill, and provide valuable feedback that will help your employees get out of the building more quickly and safely. Some fire departments will present on-site employee training in the use of fire extinguishers, often giving everyone a chance to participate in some hands-on practice.

A tour of your building and grounds by fire officials provides an opportunity for them to meet with your emergency response personnel and become more familiar with your facilities. They may also request a drawing of your building indicating all entrances and exits, the location of gas and electric shut-offs, elevators, stairwells, and fire alarm panels. These steps help firefighters preplan responses to emergencies that occur at your organization.

Many local police agencies offer a security inspection service. They will work with you and your security staff to review building security measures and alarm reliability and effectiveness and make suggestions for improvements. A building exterior inspection that includes checking for possible entry points will be conducted. The inspection may also include identifying places outside the building where vision is obstructed by trees or bushes and areas needing improved lighting. The police department will offer advice to help reduce employee theft and make presentations to staff on security and safety. Officers will also offer suggestions for arranging your front desk area for better security and help in determining the best location for a panic button or silent alarm.

There is also help at the federal government level. Check the Federal Emergency Management Agency's (FEMA) Web site for information and downloadable forms and publications, and be sure to request a catalog of their free printed material related to preparing for and responding to disasters.

Work with representatives of your facilities, security, engineering and other appropriate departments to identify areas where emergency professionals can be of help to you. Then give your local agencies a call to learn exactly what services they provide and how they can work with your organization to help prevent emergencies and improve response when emergencies happen.

Cooperation, both with your fellow employees and with outside specialists, will result in a safer and more secure working environment for everyone.

CHAPTER 3

BEING PREPARED

DISASTER CAN STRIKE QUICKLY AND WITHOUT NOTICE, and if it has not already, a serious emergency or a disaster is likely to occur at your company at some time in the future. While we often think in terms of major disasters such as terrorist attacks, hurricanes, tornadoes, earthquakes, and floods that create havoc and impact whole communities, your organization's disaster may be a smaller scale, non-headline-generating occurrence—a power outage or water main break in your immediate area, fire in one room of your building, a bomb threat, or a workplace violence incident. Just as it is not possible to totally prevent most disasters and emergencies, it is not realistic to assume that all emergencies will happen to other organizations but not to yours. Being prepared is both ethically correct and good business.

The first step in addressing security and safety threats, emergencies, and disasters should come well before the event occurs—eliminating hazards or lessening the impact of the next disaster through mitigation.

Mitigating Threats

Mitigation, the cornerstone of emergency management, is defined as an ongoing program of actions taken to reduce or eliminate the probability of a disaster occurring or to minimize the effects of those disasters that cannot be prevented. Mitigation efforts are categorized as structural, dealing primarily with building construction and location, or nonstructural, focusing on building interior and contents. Mitigation ranges from simple housekeeping and maintenance, including keeping hallways free of obstructions, bolting heavy storage units to walls, and not using telephone closets and computer rooms as storage rooms, to major steps such as engineering and seismically retrofitting buildings in areas where earthquakes are a threat or even constructing a new office building away from floodplains.

In the past, mitigation efforts have often accounted for a relatively small percentage of emergency management activities. Recent years have seen a change in this approach. In both the government and business sectors there has been a growing realization that an aggressive mitigation program can help reduce the potential for injuries and prevent some emergencies while effectively reducing the costs associated with emergencies and disasters.

Mitigation requires taking a new look at the organization's physical plant, critical operations, and support systems. It involves identifying potential hazards and assessing current risks, whether the threats are natural, technological, or incited (human). The next step is to determine what can be done now to eliminate or lessen damage and loss when future disasters occur and make improvements and changes to address the most likely threats and hazards.

Here are some questions that may help identify mitigation steps that can be initiated by your organization. If you do not know the answers to these questions, find and talk with the people in your organization who do.

- ❑ Is there a formal ongoing hazard mitigation and/or safety inspection program?
- ❑ Do existing mitigation measures including keeping hallways, doorways, and stairwells free from obstructions that may create death traps in the event of an evacuation?
- ❑ Are computers equipped with an uninterrupted power supply (UPS)?
- ❑ Are all hazardous materials stored properly?
- ❑ Have emergency generators been installed, and if so, do you and others involved in responding to emergencies know exactly what the generators will power and for how long?
- ❑ Are coffeemakers connected to timers that automatically shut them off at the end of the workday to avoid possibly causing a fire?

A negative response to any of these questions may indicate a need for some changes.

Ideally, mitigation is an enterprise-wide issue. Whether or not that is the case at your organization, everyone can get involved in hazard mitigation. For all employees mitigation is as simple as following established safety and security guidelines and policies and encouraging others to do the same. In some cases, mitigation involves noting nonstructural hazards that need to be corrected and reporting them to the appropriate person or department for corrective action. While mitigating threats may not be included in everyone's (or maybe not anyone's) official job description, it is important that all employees get involved and assist with the important ongoing process of identifying potential threats and helping to eliminate them or lessen their impact. Here are just a few of the steps all employees can take to help.

❑ Report any and all potential hazards, suspicious behavior, or unknown persons on the organization's premises.

❑ When you see an exit sign that is not lighted or when you notice a frayed electrical cord, report it in writing to the appropriate person and follow up to make certain the correction is made.

❑ Keep work areas free of an accumulation of excessive paper.

❑ Avoid storing heavy objects on high open shelves.

❑ Keep file cabinet drawers closed.

❑ Avoid putting items in corridors and exits even temporarily.

❑ Avoid stacking items on upper shelves of storage or filing units that will obstruct sprinkler devices; sprinkler devices require an 18-inch clearance.

❑ When you enter a secured building or area, do not piggyback and do not allow others, even people you know, to do so.

For better physical safety, work with security and facilities staff to enforce a policy to keep storage rooms, telephone and utility closets, boiler rooms, computer rooms, etc., locked. These areas should be accessible to employees only on an as-needed basis and should be off-limits to visitors and other outsiders.

By reducing through mitigation the effects of potential disasters that may occur, the response phase may be much more effective and result in fewer injuries to people and less damage to property.

Recovery time can be decreased significantly as a result of a comprehensive mitigation process. This will mean that the organization can be back in full operation much more quickly following a disaster, which will result in a decreased negative impact on employees, customers, clients, and the organization's financial position.

Employee Preparedness

I once heard a wise person say, "The time to start worrying is when things are going well." While worrying and fretting about future emergencies and disasters is not a productive course of action, the time to start preparing for them is when things are going well, before threats to safety and security rear their ugly heads.

To be truly effective, an emergency management program requires that all employees be knowledgeable about plans and procedures and that they participate in the emergency management program. Each employee should have a printed copy of the emergency procedures at their workspace and review them regularly, participate in scheduled training, and know the emergency response team members in their work area. Everyone should be familiar with their primary and alternate evacuation routes and outside assembly area, and it's a good idea to actually walk the evacuation route periodically so that all employees remain familiar with how they are to exit the building. Keeping a three-day supply of needed medications or medical devices at the workplace is essential should a disaster result in employees not being able to go home as scheduled.

Having well-developed and *regularly practiced* evacuation plans in place is more essential now than ever before. This is especially true in large or high-rise building and complex structures. An important factor in maximizing the safety of employees and visitors is an enforced policy that requires all employees from the mail room to the executive offices to participate fully in all evacuation drills. Granted, security and safety preparedness measures may not always be convenient. While having to stop work on an important project with a looming deadline or being interrupted in the middle of a meeting to attend emergency training or participate in an evacuation drill may be viewed as an unwelcome nuisance, everyone's participation is necessary in order to maintain an effective emergency response program.

Work with HR, security, and others at your organization to consider the value of adding some additional steps to help ensure that all employees are prepared for whatever emergencies may come your way. Make safety, security, and emergency response an agenda item at every department meeting. Include articles in organization newsletters. Post signs and information relating to safety, security, and emergency response in coffee and break rooms, cafeterias, and other areas where employees congregate.

Emergency Communication

When a major disaster occurs, being able to communicate is critical and often challenging. This may be a result either of problems with the communications systems—

telephone, fax, e-mail—or of a lack of sufficient communication plans—having established procedures and people assigned to deliver the necessary information to the appropriate people in a timely manner.

Following the World Trade Center terrorist attack key telephone and data networks and cellular antennas in Lower Manhattan were crippled. The overloaded system and damage to the communications infrastructure severely limited telephone communication. Most organizations tried in vain to use their traditional phone systems and the cell phone services provided by multiple providers. Telephone systems have vulnerabilities, and the generally accepted assumption, "God provides the dial tone," is not true. In a disaster situation there is no absolute guarantee that we will be able to place and complete a call each time we pick up the phone.

When asked to identify the best type of communication to have available for use following a disaster occurrence, my response is always, "As many as possible." Each type of communication has advantages and disadvantages, and what will and will not work cannot be predicted.

Several years ago cellular phones were considered the ideal solution for communicating following a disaster. That was before cell phones were almost as common as standard phones. Today it seems that everyone between the ages of ten and one hundred has a cell phone, and it is likely that getting a dial tone on a cell phone following a disaster of any magnitude is problematic. Today a disaster communications plan must include multiple ways to connect with others.

Start with the basics: your day-to-day telephone system and cell phones. Keep a few plain old telephones at your location. Known as "pots," these phones do not require an electrical outlet in addition to the phone outlet. They have no bells or whistles, won't dial for you, and have no caller ID or other special features, but they will work at times when newer, high-tech phones will not. To accommodate pots, add telephone jacks that bypass the switchboard and any automated telephone systems, and keep a record of the location and telephone numbers of these lines. Fax lines may also use a regular dial-tone line and bypass the switchboard, giving you additional lines for these low-tech instruments. When your primary phone system won't work because of a technology failure or power outage, pull the plain old phones out of storage and use them to maintain critical communication.

Some organizations are now purchasing satellite phones as an additional redundant emergency communication system. The cost of satellite phones has decreased over recent years. Though prices still do not make it financially feasible for most organizations to purchase and maintain more than a limited number of satellite phones, it is possible to use this technology to maintain minimal communication, e.g., for emergency calls or calls between company locations.

Pay phones may work when others do not. While the number of pay phones has continued to decrease since the introduction of cellular phones, one or more may be located in or near your building. If so, note their locations and, if possible, learn the telephone numbers. If you do have access to pay phones, keep some change in your desk as part of your emergency supplies.

Pagers and two-way radios or walkie-talkies are primarily an alternate means of internal communication that may work for your organization.

Whatever communication options are available at your organization, keep a complete and up-to-date list of all available backup communication systems, including locations and numbers.

When all else fails, use messengers. Often called "runners," these individuals deliver information between people at your facility the old fashioned way—they walk from one point to another to deliver written or verbal communication. They may also carry messages between locations by car, bicycle, or on foot.

When an emergency or disaster happens, avoid using the telephone except when absolutely necessary to report an emergency or to request assistance. There is a natural tendency to get on the phone to notify others about the emergency you've just experienced, discuss in detail what happened, or check the well-being of others. Remember that your call is helping to overload phone circuits and perhaps preventing other, more important—even life-saving—calls from going through.

Rather than everyone making phone calls to share information, a good source for the latest status reports, and in the case of widespread disasters, updates from government agencies and public safety officials, is tuning in to local radio or television stations. When a disaster occurs, local media typically provide ongoing coverage until the situation is under control.

While the technology of disaster communication is extremely important, it is equally important to consider with whom we need to maintain communication, how that will be done, and who will have the responsibility for doing so.

Employees, customers, clients, and other stakeholders are any organization's most important asset in normal conditions and doubly so in a disaster situation. In the event of a major emergency or disaster, it is important that the organization make every effort to provide employees with information concerning external conditions that may affect their families, homes, and ability to travel safely. Knowing that employees are safe and being of aware of their location is essential. Keeping them informed of the situation and when and where they are to report to work following an interruption of operations is critical.

Customers and clients need to know that your organization will still be able to meet their needs by delivering your product or service. Quickly notifying key customers and clients, and vendors and suppliers of your organization's situation and how well you are handling an emergency or disaster is vital.

The traditional emergency notification process has been a call tree—a person begins the call tree by calling two or three employees. Each of them calls two or three more employees until everyone in the organization has been reached. While this method can be effective, it is only as strong as its weakest "branch." The unavailability of a person or persons on the tree or outdated contact information on telephone lists can result in some employees not receiving important information.

An alternate means of communication with employees following a disaster that many organizations use successfully is a communication provider for a toll-free message line with multiple mailboxes and remote recording capability. Organizations with two or more locations can locate the toll-free line in an out-of-area facility, and those with a single location or with all facilities in a small geographic area can contract with a communication provider for the toll-free service. Following a disaster, when making a call between two phone numbers within an area may be extremely difficult, the toll-free remote service can facilitate communications between the organization and its employees, and perhaps even employees' families. Employees can contact this number for updates on the emergency situation, information on when and where to report for work, or other important communications. In addition, families may leave messages on this line to be relayed to employees in the field or those unable to get home because of road conditions or the need to stay at work. Responsibility for updating the outgoing messages as necessary is assigned to emergency response personnel, an HR representative, or other staff person. Employees are also assigned to retrieve and relay messages to on-duty employees as required.

Managers and supervisors can prepare to help maintain critical employee communication in the aftermath of a serious emergency or disaster by maintaining a current personnel roster, including home telephone numbers and cell phone numbers, and keeping a copy both at work and at home.

Some organizations have opted to use automated notification systems. These range from the older standard auto-dialers to state-of-the-art systems that utilize computerized systems to automate emergency notifications by voice, pager, fax, and e-mail and even verify receipt of information by prompting message recipients for a response.

Whatever notification and communication systems and procedures your organization has in place, be familiar with the disaster communications plans and know what your role is in the post-emergency communication process. What are you expected to do to keep employees, customers, clients, and others informed about the situation? If you are responsible for relaying information, who will advise you what information you are to pass along and to whom? Do you have a regularly updated list of contact information for those people with whom you are to communicate? For those outside the organization the list should include office phone number, mobile phone, work e-mail address, and pager numbers. For employees also add home telephone number, personal e-mail address, and perhaps the number of an alternate home location (week-end or vacation home).

In a disaster situation, providing accurate information in a timely manner helps prevent the gaps being filled in with rumors, gossip, and half-truths.

Disaster Supplies and Equipment

When a disaster occurs, actions that protect the safety and welfare of employees and visitors are the most critical, followed by steps to secure the building. In an area-wide disaster, it may be impossible for law enforcement, the fire department, and medical professionals to immediately respond to all requests for assistance. If the disaster causes severe damage to roads, streets, and bridges, emergency units may temporarily be unable to reach your location. It is also possible that the same circumstances that prevent public safety agencies from reaching your building may necessitate employees having to stay at the work location until the immediate danger has passed and streets and roadways have been cleared or repaired. The planning standard for major disasters is to prepare to be self-sufficient for at least seventy-two hours. This makes being equipped to respond internally to handle life- and property-threatening situations essential.

Emergency supplies and equipment may be divided into four basic categories: first-aid supplies, emergency equipment, supplies for sheltering in place, and evacuation equipment. The emergency supplies and equipment needed at your location will be based on the number of employees and the type of operation. For example, the needs of a manufacturing operation employing several hundred people will vary greatly from the needs of an accounting firm with seventy employees. Other factors to take into account are the number of visitors or customers typically in the building at any one time, as well as the types of emergencies and disasters your organization is most likely to experience.

While most organizations maintain standard first-aid kits containing band-aids, aspirin, alcohol or peroxide, gauze, adhesive tape, and cotton balls, an expanded list of supplies and equipment is required to meet today's needs. Among the items that should be included in your first-aid supplies are multiple types and sizes of bandages, cardboard and wire splints, splinter forceps, sterile water pouches, eye pads, scissors, liquid antibacterial hand soap, and garbage bags. A good basic first-aid handbook is also essential.

Examples of emergency supplies are water purification tablets, duct tape, plastic sheeting, flashlights and batteries, light sticks, markers and notepads, and basic tools.

If the organization opts to form and train search and rescue teams, necessary extrication and evacuation equipment will include sturdy work gloves, dust masks, axes, crowbars, nylon rope, hard hats and protective clothing.

In addition to food and water, long-term sheltering in place may require items including blankets, a hand-operated can opener, a battery-operated radio with extra batteries, cups, pots to boil water, and toilet tissue.

The decision as to whether to stock and maintain a three-day supply of food and water for all employees is a policy issue. Many organizations find that they have an adequate supply of water (and other beverages) in water coolers, break rooms, and the cafeteria. In buildings where there is an on-site cafeteria, the food supply there may be adequate. Also check to see how much food is contained in on-site vending machines. Vending machine food may not be gourmet, but it will suffice until people can leave the building.

The Red Cross and local emergency agencies can provide you with detailed lists of suggested equipment and supplies. As with all elements of emergency preparedness, standard equipment and supplies lists must be adjusted and tailored to fit the organization's specific needs.

Once a decision is made about what to keep on hand, responsibility must be assigned for maintaining the supplies and equipment. Emergency supplies of food and water and some first-aid supplies have expiration dates. All first-aid supplies and equipment must be inventoried and restocked no less than annually and preferably twice annually, as well as after each emergency event.

Desk Emergency Kit

Employees can keep some simple items at their work station that will be invaluable should disaster strike. The first of these is a readily available, easy-to-read list of emergency numbers. This should include 9-1-1 and the numbers for the organization's security staff, the emergency response team leader for the floor or area, nearest first-aid/CPR-trained employee(s), personal physician, and hospital or medical care facility of choice, as well as home and family emergency numbers.

Keep a flashlight handy in the event of a power outage. You'll also want to have at least two sets of extra batteries and replace them if they are not used within six months.

If you wear shoes to work that are not comfortable for walking or climbing stairs, keep a comfortable pair of shoes at your work station. Some coins for pay phones and vending machines may also come in handy.

Training, Drills, and Exercises

Just having a plan is not enough.

Perhaps the most important aspect of safety, security, and emergency management is to develop awareness through training. The first step is to provide all employees with an orientation covering all aspects of the emergency management program. This can be accomplished by a formal training program, periodic briefings by managers, or a video tape that describes the organization's emergency management program. Include an introduction to the emergency management program as part of new employee orientation.

The key to a successful safety and security program is the appropriate level of training for all employees and a schedule of drills and exercises that provides an opportunity for practicing emergency procedures and making certain that plans will function as expected in real world events. ERTs are required by local code or ordinance in some locations, and in some cases ERT training is specified by OSHA (Occupational Safety and Health Administration) regulations as well as generally accepted standards of training. When there are regulations and standards, not adhering to them may create a legal liability.

While every emergency situation is unique, this does not mean that there is no value in testing procedures and training people through a well-planned program of drills and exercises. Athletes practice even though no two games are identical. Actors rehearse even though no two performances of a play will be exactly the same. The military trains before going into battle even though each battle is different from all others. Yet without that practice, rehearsing, and training, the level of performance in the actual event would at best be chaotic and at worst result in utter failure. The same is true with emergency training and drills. The Chinese proverb, "I hear and I forget; I see and I remember; I do and I understand," applies as employees gain a true understanding of what to do in emergencies by rehearsing.

We all began participating in fire drills in our elementary school days, and the drills are as important today in our work environment as they were back then. These evacuation drills, often required by local agencies, are an essential step in training all employees to respond to emergencies.

While developing plans and procedures is a critical element of emergency preparedness, and the one typically given the most time and thought, without drills and exercises to test our plans, we may be creating a false sense of security. Without testing, we may find that our emergency procedures, which look great on paper, will not work when put into action and might even result in more harm being done.

The best emergency procedures ever developed have no value unless all employees are aware of what the mutual expectations are when a disaster occurs—what they are to do and what the organization will do—through regularly scheduled training and refreshers.

Drills and exercises also provide a logical time to test alarm and communication systems to make sure they are functioning as expected. It is not uncommon that employees of some organizations have never experienced an alarm activation, and a drill is the perfect time to familiarize employees with audible and visual fire alarm and alert and warning systems.

Through the understanding of the emergency procedures that employees gain by participating in drills, evacuation times are shortened, employees are more confident in their actions, and improvements are realized with each evacuation drill or emergency exercise that is conducted.

To take preparedness to the next level and provide a training opportunity for those with specific emergency responsibilities, a tabletop exercise, also known as a desktop exercise, paper exercise, or walkthrough, can be added to your emergency preparedness training and testing schedule. Tabletop Exercises to help you practice various situations are included in Appendix 5.

With an ongoing cycle of training, drills, and exercises, followed by corrections and enhancements, the organization's emergency plans and procedures and employee emergency response capabilities will continue to improve.

Once there is knowledge of the organization's existing policies, plans, and procedures and complete understanding of the overall approach to addressing emergencies, disasters, and security and safety threats, a more complete picture of the emergency management role of the front desk professional begins to emerge. It is now possible to better understand the importance of the front desk professional's handling of emergencies, threats, and unexpected situations.

CHAPTER 4

WHAT TO DO WHEN

AS A RESULT OF THE EVENTS OF SEPTEMBER 11, 2001, safety and security planning changed and began to focus on terror-related threats, and appropriately so. The very history of the United States is now divided into two eras: before September 11 and after September 11. While it is essential that we prepare to respond to terrorist acts, we must also continue to address the more common safety and security situations that can threaten employees, facilities, and operations.

The following pages contain guidelines for what to when. . .any one of a variety of emergencies and disasters occurs. Long-standing threats including fire, medical emergencies, and building evacuation, and the new threats of our millennium, such as terrorist attacks, shootings, and receipt of suspicious mail, are included.

Before implementing these procedures, be certain that they adhere to your organization's policies and existing emergency management plans and that they are in alignment with guidelines established by local public safety officials.

Each organization is unique, and that uniqueness must be reflected in all areas of the operation, including response to emergencies and safety and security threats. As an example of the need to tailor procedures I always recall one high-tech company where I assisted with the development of an emergency preparedness and response program.

Company policy allowed employees to bring pets to work, and they did. Mostly dogs, also a few birds, cats, and fish, and even an occasional rabbit, reptile, or rodent. To make sure that this unusual group of building inhabitants was taken care of in an emergency, a "pets" section was included in the company's emergency preparedness and response plan. Procedures outlined the requirement that each employee having a pet with them at work when an emergency occurred take full and complete responsibility for their animal and included a requirement that pet owners keep an emergency supply of pet food, a leash or carrier, a copy of the pet's license, and veterinarian contact information at the workplace.

While your organization may not need to address issues that are quite as out of the ordinary as this example, there are likely other factors, perhaps a remote location, unique building configuration, or large numbers of visitors or customers on premises daily, that will require taking additional preparedness steps or tailoring emergency procedures.

Every emergency and every disaster situation is different, and the requirements for what needs to be done to respond may vary greatly. Circumstances may require thinking outside the box, being flexible, and using creativity. Nothing in written plans and procedures should ever preclude or override the exercise of prudent judgment and common sense.

We begin with the specific steps to follow for the four emergency procedures you are likely to use more than any others:

- ❏   How to call 9-1-1
- ❏   How to respond to medical emergencies
- ❏   What to do when there is a fire
- ❏   How to evacuate the building

Procedures for technological emergencies—hazardous materials accidents and power outages—are included. There are several disaster types that fall into the incited disasters category. Of these intentional human acts, violent incidents in the workplace, terrorism, and bomb threats are included.

You will also find these procedures in an easy-to-use checklist format in Appendix 3.

Procedures for geographic-specific natural disasters (e.g., hurricane, tornado, tsunami, earthquake, and flood) are not included. As when discussing many other subjects, there is an 80/20 rule that applies to responding to emergencies. In emergency response the 80/20 rule is that the steps taken to respond to any emergency are the same steps necessary to respond to 80 per cent of all emergencies with the remaining 20 percent of steps to be taken specific to a given emergency or disaster. For example, when a natural disaster occurs, be it a hurricane, earthquake, or flood, the ERT will be activated and many of the basic emergency procedures will be implemented—call 9-1-1, respond to medical emergencies, or possibly evacuate the building.

To add procedures for the natural disasters that may impact your location, check your organization's emergency plans or contact local public safety officials or the Red Cross for the procedures to follow.

Calling 9-1-1

To call for assistance in most emergency situations, you will call 9-1-1, which is set for automatic dial on most telephones. In most cases a call to 9-1-1 is received by a dispatcher in a central location (dispatch center), often equipped with sophisticated computerized equipment that handles calls for public safety agencies—fire, police, emergency medical professionals. A dispatcher receives a call, gathers the needed information, determines the type of help that is needed, and dispatches the appropriate available response units to your location. The dispatcher also relays critical information to the responding units while they are en route so they can actually begin to prepare to take immediate action once they arrive at the emergency scene. Once you have dialed 9-1-1, there are specific steps you can follow to assist the person receiving the call to get the quickest and most effective response.

First rule—never assume that someone else had made the call. If you are not certain that 9-1-1 has been called, call it yourself or *directly* instruct someone else to do so. It is better by far to risk the call's being made twice than to risk its not having been made at all. When calling 9-1-1, stay calm and speak slowly and clearly. Provide information that is to the point. Avoid giving unnecessary information. If you find that you are talking too fast, simply stop for a second, take a deep breath, and begin again.

Follow the dispatcher's lead and be prepared to give the following information. Start with your name. Give the nature of the emergency—injury, violent incident, fire, hazardous material spill, etc. Though highly computerized dispatch centers can likely identify your location and the telephone number from which you are calling, provide your complete location information, including the street address, nearest cross street, and best entrance to use. Providing complete location information is especially important if you are calling from a cell phone as the location of cell phones cannot be identified. Give the exact location in the building where the incident has occurred, "Third floor; Conference Room A, to the right as you exit the elevator." Provide your phone number in the event that you are cut off or the dispatcher needs to call you back. If you are not in danger, stay on the line until the dispatcher tells you to hang up or disconnects. In some cases you will be asked to provide additional information (e.g., updates on the situation, details about the ill or injured person) that will be relayed to emergency responders while they are en route to your location. In cases of medical emergencies, the dispatcher may give you instructions for what to do for the victim until the medical unit arrives.

It may seem that the dispatcher is keeping you on the line for an extremely long time. Don't be concerned. Keep in mind that while they are talking with you, gathering the necessary information, and asking you questions or giving you instructions, they have already dispatched emergency equipment and personnel. Help is on the way.

If a building evacuation has not been ordered, send someone to meet the emergency responders at the entrance and, if necessary, have someone secure an elevator on the main floor for responders and assign another person to meet them at the elevator or at the top of the stairway on the destination floor to lead them to their exact destination.

These simple steps can avoid unnecessary delays and help the emergency professionals begin providing the greatest help in the shortest time.

A final thought to consider when you call 9-1-1. At the time of an emergency or disaster, our perception of time becomes distorted. It is not uncommon to hear someone at the scene of an emergency say that the fire department or ambulance took almost an hour to get there, only to learn from a review of taped dispatch radio transmissions that units arrived within a quarter of an hour or less after the call was made. As you make the call to 9-1-1, you may want to take a look at a clock or your watch and note the time to help you keep a realistic perspective on the time factor.

Medical Emergency or Injury

The most likely type of emergency to which you will respond is a medical emergency, either an illness or an injury. Medical emergencies and accidents range from an employee who has suffered a minor cut to the hand to a visitor who is experiencing chest pains and having difficulty breathing. If you are the first person to reach the ill or injured person, get help. If you are not first-aid trained, call out for someone who is. Direct someone to phone 9-1-1 to request that emergency medical personnel respond. Have someone else notify security.

Do no harm. Do not attempt to give any medical treatment for which you are not trained and qualified. If the person is not conscious, look, listen, and feel for breathing. If you have some basic skills, feel for a pulse. If there is bleeding, attempt to control it by applying direct pressure to the wound with your fingers or hand until a clean dressing is available. Do not move the ill or injured person unless not doing so may result in further injury. Remain calm. Reassure the ill or injured person and show genuine concern. Let them know that medical help is on the way and that you will stay with them until medical professionals get there. Keep the victim warm with a blanket, jacket, or coat. Do not give anything to eat or drink. In emergency situations, crowds of concerned people often gather to see if they can help or just because they are curious. Not only is being the center of attention very disconcerting to the ill or injured person, those gathered can get in the way of responding emergency personnel. Have security keep people away from the victim and out of the area or designate someone else to do so.

Once the ill or injured person has received treatment or been transported to a medical facility, report the incident in writing as specified by your organization's emergency procedures. If the person is to be transported to the hospital, obtain their name, phone number, and intended destination, and make all reports as required by organization policies and emergency procedures.

If the injury involved bodily fluid, keep others out of the area and notify facilities to arrange for clean-up.

Fire

Training and practice before a fire occurs are essential. Every employee needs to know the evacuation procedures and routes for their area. Those trained in the use of fire extinguishers should know the locations of extinguishers in their area.

When a fire occurs, time is of the essence. Every minute is critical and may mean the difference between a fire that is an inconvenience to the organization and its employees and a fire that is a disaster. Whether the fire is a minor fire contained in one room or a quickly spreading fire that threatens the entire building, certain basic rules always apply.

First and most important, remove people from danger. Sound the alarm and yell out a warning to evacuate for any fire, large or small. This will activate ERT members who will assist with the building evacuation. Use established evacuation procedures to get all employees and visitors out of the building. If it's safe to do so, call 9-1-1 before evacuating, even though the fire alarm has been activated.

Before opening any door, place a hand one inch from the door near the top to see if it is hot. If you feel heat, fire or smoke is on the other side and the door should not be opened. Open closed doors slowly and be prepared to close them quickly at the first sign of fire.

If there is a lot of smoke, follow the old firefighter's adage, "Stay low and stay alive." Crawl on your hands and knees or duck-walk toward the emergency exit using walls to guide you. This makes breathing easier. If possible place a damp cloth or handkerchief over your nose and mouth.

If clothing catches fire, the procedure we all learned in elementary school still applies—stop, drop, and roll.

When exiting the building, watch for falling debris and be careful not to trip over fire equipment or on wet surfaces. Never go back into a burning building for any reason.

The second step is to contain the spread of fire. Close windows as you exit and close, but do not lock, doors after everyone has exited. This will help slow the fire's progress.

Based on the size of the fire and how quickly it is spreading, determine whether or not to use an extinguisher to fight the fire. While using a fire extinguisher is not at all complicated and can be easily learned, if you have not received training, do not attempt to use one to fight the fire.

If you have received training, consider the following:

❑   Has the alarm been sounded and is the evacuation in progress?

❑   Is the fire small and contained?

❑   Can you fight the fire without encountering smoky conditions?

❑   Will you still be able to exit the area safely without exposure to fire?

Only if you can answer yes to all these questions should you consider using a fire extinguisher.

My suggestion is this: If you have even the least bit of discomfort or uncertainty about your answers to any of the above questions, close the door and get out. If the fire is larger than a wastebasket and is spreading, forget the fire extinguisher, and get out. Let the professionals do the job for which they have been trained and for which they have the needed protective gear and equipment.

Building Evacuation

When an evacuation is ordered, either through activation of the fire alarm, by employees being verbally alerted by ERT members, or at the direction of public safety officials, all employees should immediately evacuate the building. In some facilities there is a tendency on the part of some employees to question whether it is really necessary to evacuate or if perhaps the alarm was activated as part of an evacuation drill or was a false alarm. Regardless, it should be a firm policy that is understood by all employees, that without exception everyone is to evacuate the building immediately when an alarm sounds.

If an evacuation is ordered for a bomb threat, carefully check your work area before leaving and report any unusual package or other material to security or an ERT member. Do not touch any suspicious packages.

When evacuation is ordered, to the extent time allows, secure any sensitive documents or valuables, shut down computers and other equipment, take personal belongings, and follow instructions of the ERT. Move quickly but do not run toward to the nearest emergency exit and assist any visitors to do the same. Do not use elevators; stay to the right in hallways and stairways; avoid talking unnecessarily and be as quiet as possible so emergency instructions may be heard.

Proceed to your designated outdoor assembly area and check in with your manager, supervisor, or other designated person. It is important to stay in the assembly area until you are released. Leaving the area before you are released may lead to uncertainty about your safety and whereabouts.

Department managers, supervisors, or others as designated in the organization's emergency procedures will account for all personnel present at the time of evacuation. Any missing person, including their last known location, should be reported immediately to the assembly area coordinator.

During an evacuation of the building, if there are pre-designated emergency response teams, team members have full authority over response by occupants on the assigned floor or area. Follow all directions given by public safety officials, ERT members, security staff, or over public address system. Avoid unnecessary talking and noise so emergency instructions may be heard. As in any emergency, remember to remain calm and don't panic. Your behavior helps set the tone for others.

ERT members will direct employees and visitors to the fire exits and stairwells and provide or obtain first-aid treatment for the injured. The team includes searchers. Working in pairs, searchers will systematically search their assigned area to be certain everyone heard the alarm and has left the area.

In the front desk area make sure all visitors calmly evacuate using the closest emergency exit. If time permits, power down computers and shut down equipment in accordance with established procedures.

Remind everyone, "Do not use elevators." While these instructions may seem like an unnecessary restatement of something everyone knows, in an emergency situation there will be those who head straight for an elevator just as there will be people who attempt to get to the door through which they entered the building to leave rather than going to their pre-assigned emergency exit.

When going down stairways, do not run, walk. Keep to the right and allow those from lower floors to blend in with those already in the stairwell.

Once out of the building, no one should return for any reason until an all clear is issued by public safety officials.

A critical last step in the evacuation process is accounting for all personnel and visitors to be certain that everyone made it out of the building safely. Each employee should go directly to their pre-assigned outdoor assembly area and report in to the assembly area coordinator for their group. Everyone should stay in their assembly area to await further instructions—either to return to the building or to be released by the assembly area coordinator to leave.

Power Outage

Power outages may be caused by lightning storms, ice on power lines, natural disasters including tornadoes, hurricanes, or earthquakes, or an excessive demand on the power supply. The duration of a power outage may be only minutes or it may be days. Some organizations have installed emergency generators that will power the entire operation for several hours or a few days. Others have opted to have battery back-up only for life safety systems and perhaps critical equipment.

If you are not familiar with the emergency power capabilities in your building, talk with facilities or engineering to learn what in the front desk area will, and will not, be powered by emergency generators.

When there is a power outage, get your flashlight. Calm and reassure any visitors and fellow employees who may be nearby. If there are window coverings, open them to allow any available natural light into the building. Encourage people to stay where they rather than trying to reach other areas of the building or leaving in the dark. Power down or shut off computers and shut off other equipment to avoid damage when the power is restored.

Wait for instructions from security, facilities, or HR. Once there is more information about the expected duration of the power outage, a decision will be made and announced as to whether people should wait for the power to be restored or leave the building. The time of day is also a factor.

Bomb Threat

Law enforcement authorities find that revenge and a desire to disrupt an organization's operations are the motivation behind the majority of bomb threats. The caller may want to create an atmosphere of fear, anxiety, or panic. Perpetrators of these threats may be a former employee or business partner, a dissatisfied former client or customer, or an angry spouse or girl/boyfriend. Although most bomb threats are hoaxes, in some cases, the threat is real and the caller wants to minimize personal injury and/or property damage by providing advanced warning that an explosive device has been placed. Whatever the motivation and regardless of who is making the bomb threat, take all threatening or malicious telephone calls, facsimiles, or e-mails seriously until a complete investigation conclusively proves otherwise.

Threats are most frequently received by telephone, but they may also be delivered through the mail. No single course of action will always be suitable in a bomb threat situation. Each situation and the validity of each threat must be evaluated by public safety and security specialists in order to determine what actions should be taken.

If you receive a phoned bomb threat, stay calm and attempt to keep the caller on the line as long as possible. If you have caller ID, note the telephone number. Complete a bomb threat checklist that provides a set list of questions to ask the caller. These range from questions requiring very basic responses such as "What is your name?" to the more complex "Why are you doing this?" (A sample bomb threat checklist, based on the FBI's standard checklist, is contained in the emergency procedures checklists, Appendix 3.) If possible, while caller is still on the line, activate a silent alarm or motion to someone nearby that you are receiving a bomb threat and to call 9-1-1. As soon as the caller hangs up, if 9-1-1 has not been called, do so immediately or ask someone to make the call. Also notify security, facilities, and any others as outlined in the organization's emergency response procedures.

Once a phoned bomb threat has been received, there are options:

1. Immediately evacuate everyone, then search for a bomb.
2. Evacuate some employees and visitors while a search is undertaken.
3. Evacuate no one and conduct a search.

Deciding which of these options to adopt for your organization is a policy decision. While some organizations, based on the information gathered from the bomb threat checklist, do not necessarily automatically evacuate (e.g., a company that regularly receives threats from an identifiable person or persons, a nonprofit organization that receives bomb threats daily, high schools on the first day of finals or on Friday morning), when there is any question, my preference is always for option number 1—immediately evacuate everyone, then conduct a search.

Other threats may be received in writing. If this happens, call 9-1-1 and security immediately. Save all packaging materials and the envelope or other container. If it is not obvious, try to remember or find out how it was delivered, e.g., by postal service, delivery service or courier, or hand carried by an individual. Until law enforcement officials arrive, avoid handling the items as any handwriting, fingerprints, and postmarks will be used as evidence in tracking and identifying the individual sending the threat.

If the responsible officials determine that the building should be evacuated in response to a threat, open doors and windows to allow the pressure of a blast to escape if a bomb does go off. Do not use walkie-talkies, cell phones, pagers, or other devices that may trigger detonation of an explosive device. Evacuate as directed and as outlined in your organization's evacuation procedures. If you notice a suspicious item, immediately notify security or public safety officials if they have arrived. Never move or touch any suspicious item.

Some organizations establish a special alarm or signal for an evacuation in response to a bomb threat. Others may elect to not announce the reason for the evacuation before or even after the evacuation to avoid panic. As with other emergency response issues, these are policy decisions to be made by management.

Check now with your local police and fire departments about their bomb search policies. Will they do the search? Will they request that one or more persons from your organization assist? (Assistance from an employee who is very familiar with the normal sights, sounds, and smell of the building is extremely helpful during a bomb search.) In some areas both police and fire units respond. While the police conduct the search, fire units stay a prescribed distance away from the building. People seeing this standard procedure for the first time may be quite surprised at the distance maintained by fire units until they understand that maintaining this distance ensures that firefighters will be available to rescue people and put out fires should there be an explosion.

Hazardous Materials Incident

A hazardous material is a substance or combination of substances that, because of quantity, concentration, or physical or chemical characteristics, may pose a potential hazard to humans or the environment. A hazardous materials incident may be a spill of chemicals, flammable liquids, toxic or corrosive materials, or other dangerous material inside your building, or a hazardous materials incident may be a spill on a highway or railway near your location. Of the two, it is more likely that most organizations will experience the latter.

Is your organization near railroad tracks or major highways? Is there a manufacturer using toxic chemicals or a toxic materials storage facility nearby? The answers to these questions provide some indication of the likelihood that you may be impacted by a hazardous materials spill.

If you see what may be a hazardous materials spill outside your facility, do not assume that officials have been notified. Dial 9-1-1, identify the location, and describe the situation. In such cases, fire department personnel may advise that everyone shelter in place.

Employees should close all windows and doors to the outside, and facilities or engineering may be directed to shut down the building's ventilation system. Everyone should continue to stay in the building until public safety officials advise that the incident has been resolved and that it is safe to leave. You can also monitor local radio broadcasts for instructions and updated information.

Does your company use hazardous materials in processing or manufacturing? Even though your organization may not typically store or use hazardous materials in processing or manufacturing, if any liquids or other products appear questionable, notify your supervisor, security, or facilities immediately. If a noxious odor is present, or if there is any suspected danger, evacuate all persons from the immediate area.

If there is a known or suspected suspicious substance release inside your building, leave the area immediately and advise others to do so also. Close off the area and restrict access. Dial 9-1-1, describe the situation, provide the location of the suspicious product, and describe the type of substance. What is its color? Is there an odor? It is a powder? Gas? Liquid? Listen to the instructions the dispatcher gives you. If anyone has been exposed to the substance, direct them to a safe area and restrict their contact with others. Follow all instructions given by public safety officials.

Violent Incident

There are several types of violent incidents. These include violence in the workplace, terrorism, and civil disorders. Of these, it is most likely that your organization will experience a violence in the workplace incident, one of the foremost concerns of many security directors.

Workplace Violence

The number of violent incidents in the workplace has continued to increase over the past two decades, and no type of organization, business, or government agency has been immune. It is estimated that each day thousands of threats are made against employees, and hundreds are actually attacked. These incidents may be seemingly innocent, as when one employee pushes another, or they may have a fatal outcome, ending with the death of an employee or employees. There are approximately two million violent incidents at work annually with the annual related costs to business of over $36 billion. Less tangible results of such an incident are lowered productivity and morale. These astounding facts are an indication of the importance of taking action.

Violent workplace incidents are primarily one employee attacking another employee or an employee attacking a supervisor. Though fewer in number, other violent incidents occur when a customer attacks an employee or when a boyfriend/girlfriend or spouse attacks an employee.

There are several steps that can be taken to help prevent workplace violence and to prepare a response should violence occur. The first step is to assess the seriousness of the problem in organizations similar to yours, as well as in your geographic area. At the same time, assess your organization's readiness for dealing with workplace violence. An individual or group in your organization, often HR or security, working with specialized resources can become the subject matter experts. By working with security experts, law enforcement, and counselors specializing in workplace violence, an action plan can be developed to take the necessary steps to protect people in your organization.

Policy addressing workplace violence should include the requirement that every threat of violence made, whether overt or veiled, be reported to a supervisor, manager, or HR. This requirement includes threats that are made verbally, in writing, or via e-mail. There should be no exceptions, even if it appears that the threat is being made in a seemingly joking manner. The report is made a part of the threatening employee's permanent record. This process often shows a pattern of increasing violence that can then be managed before it results in serious injury or worse.

Establishing and enforcing a proactive policy to deal with potential violence and educating managers and supervisors are two basic and critical steps. All employees should be made aware that it is their responsibility to report any and all experienced or witnessed acts of violence, potential violence, or threats of violence, or any other violations of the organization's workplace violence policy and that their identity will be protected if they so choose. Any employee who believes that they have been harassed or threatened at the workplace has a responsibility to advise the work supervisor or manager, HR, and security. Managers and supervisors have a responsibility to respond promptly to allegations of workplace violence.

To ensure that all employees are fully aware of policies regarding violence in the workplace, some organizations hold training sessions for all employees to introduce new or revised policies and enforce the training with reminders in employee newsletters or by having supervisors and managers include updates in departmental meetings.

In many cases there are early warning signs of potential violence. A history of violent behavior and verbal threats of harm are among the most obvious as are an obsession with weapons or carrying a concealed weapon. Intimidating others, instilling fear in fellow employees, showing a disregard for the safety of coworkers, or purposely breaking or damaging property are additional warning signs. Not taking criticism well or holding a grudge are also possible warning signs. Expressing extreme desperation over personal problems or feelings that the "world is against me" are also indications of potential trouble. While an employee exhibiting such behavior one time is not necessarily cause for alarm, multiple or repeated incidences of such behavior do need attention. The exception is an employee who carries a concealed weapon of any type to work even once—this requires an immediate response.

An increasing number of organizations are establishing a threat response team composed of representatives of HR and security, a workplace violence specialist, and the supervisor or manager of the employee in question. In some cases the organization's legal counsel may be included. This early review process is used to determine the most advisable course of action—do nothing and continue to monitor, counsel the employee, require violence management classes, reassign the employee to another job or department, or begin a course of action leading to the employee's dismissal. This proactive course of action serves to help prevent a serious violent action from happening.

Employees should know that they have an option to report situations in which they feel threatened by someone from outside the organization or when there is a restraining order in effect. This allows security and the front desk area to be aware of the situation and to know if there are individuals who should not have access to the building under any circumstances.

Should a violent or threatening incident occur, consider your personal safety first. Then, as possible, help others. Dial 9-1-1 at the earliest opportunity. If it is safe to do so, quietly leave the area. Attempt to notify others in the area of the threat and increase distance between yourself and the person. If possible, give a pre-arranged nonverbal signal to security or others that an incident is in progress.

Remain calm and nonthreatening. Listen to what the threatening person says and be supportive and empathetic. Do not argue, threaten, or treat the individual in any way that might be interpreted as disrespectful. Take no action that might make the person nervous as that may cause the individual to become more violent. Use the person's name, if you know it, and maintain eye contact. Get the person to sit down, if you can; remain standing if the person refuses to sit.

Keep a chair, counter, or desk between yourself and the other person. If possible, maintain a distance of three to six feet between you and the threatening person. Always try to provide yourself with at least one clear means of exit. If the person is unknown to you, note the physical description of the person (sex, age, height, weight, clothing), including any distinguishing scars or marks.

If a weapon is involved, cooperate fully with all demands. If there is money or other valuables at the front desk and if you are asked to hand it over, do so without resisting. No hesitation, no questions. Material items are not worth risking a life. Take no action that would jeopardize the safety of personnel or visitors.

Do not attempt to be a hero. Never try to grab the weapon or overpower the person. Explain any movements you make at all times. Do not make any quick moves that might result in a violent response.

In the aftermath of a violent incident, make all reports outlined in your organization's standard procedures. Work with HR to make available appropriate counseling for employees who are experiencing trauma as a result of the incident. Talk with HR and security to determine if there may be a need to add additional security measures or to temporarily or permanently increase security staff.

Civil Disturbance

Civil disturbances are situations where a person, or more typically a group of people, demonstrate to call attention to an issue or cause or purposely disrupt an organization with whose policies or operations they do not agree. Even a public event celebration that gets out of hand can end in a civil disturbance. If violence results, it is typically aimed against property, but personal assaults may also occur.

Civil disturbances often occur in areas that are natural gathering places, and the likelihood of your organization being impacted by a civil disturbance is based to a great extent on your location.

If you see or learn of a disturbance near your building, notify security at once. Based on the situation, security may restrict access to the building and have all building occupants shelter in place until danger has passed. If those participating in the disturbance enter or attempt to enter the building, remain calm and avoid provoking aggression. As quickly as possible, call 9-1-1 and security.

In the front desk area, stay calm and calm others. Even if access is not restricted, encourage everyone to stay inside until the situation is under control. Stay away from windows and exterior doors and advise others to do so. If there are window coverings in the building, close them.

If you are outside and observe a disruptive occurrence, do not argue with or in any way participants. Leave the area immediately and go inside.

Terrorist Attack

Until recent years, terrorism was thought of as something that only happened in other countries or on other continents. A book on front desk safety and security would very likely not have discussed the subject. Most people in the United States considered the 1993 bombing of the World Trade Center in New York and the 1995 bombing of the Alfred P. Murah Federal Building in Oklahoma City anomalies rather than warnings of possible future events. We now know all too well that terrorism does not occur only in far-away places. Organizations have shifted their focus, and there is now a greater emphasis on terrorism threats that severely undermine an organization's ability to protect its employees.

The FBI defines terrorism as "the unlawful use of force or violence against persons or property to intimidate or coerce a government, the civilian population, or any segment thereof, in the furtherance of political or social objectives." Terrorists are primarily interested in inflicting maximum destruction in a strictly limited period of time, and a small terrorist group is capable of inflicting damage out of proportion to its size.

Due to their high visibility, sporting events, political conventions, and prominent landmarks often serve as targets for domestic and foreign terrorist groups. Terrorists also choose targets with relatively easy public access and where detection can be avoided before and after the attack.

A building's location, prominence, access to foot and vehicular traffic, and type of occupancy influence the extent to which it may be a target for a terrorist attack. Multitenant high-rise buildings and those that house oil companies, government offices, international corporations, or controversial operations (e.g., animal testing laboratory, abortion clinic) may be at greater risk for a terrorist attack.

In the past, bombing has been the most popular method used in terrorist incidents in the United States. More recently, common weapons and tactics include explosives, kidnappings, hijackings, arson, and shootings. In addition, the potential threat of nuclear, chemical, or biological attack has been recognized.

All levels of government—local, state, and federal—began developing strategies to combat terrorism prior to the September 11, 2001, attacks on the World Trade Center and the Pentagon. However, since that time, efforts have been accelerated to prepare the general population for the possibility of additional terrorist incidents.

Terrorism falls into two categories, international (foreign-based) and domestic (non-foreign-based). Bombings and threats of biological, chemical, or nuclear agents used as weapons of mass destruction fall under the definition of international terrorism. In addition to the attacks on the World Trade Center and the Pentagon, bombings of embassies and military bases and international hostage situations are other examples of international terrorism. The mailing of powdery substances to businesses, government agencies, and nonprofit organizations to create anthrax scares, school shootings, bomb threats, and bombings are examples of domestic terrorism.

The Homeland Security Advisory System was established as a means to disseminate information regarding the risk of terrorist acts to federal, state, and local authorities and to the American people. We have become familiar with the Homeland Security Advisory System color-coded threat conditions, as shown in Figure 2, and know that code green is a low threat level while a red condition indicates an extremely high risk of attack. While the Department of Homeland Security advises us to remain vigilant, prepared, and ready at all Threat Condition levels, being more aware of the meaning of each risk condition is helpful.

Green: Low. This condition is declared when there is a low risk of terrorist attacks.

Blue: Guarded. This condition is declared when there is a general risk of terrorist attacks. At this level be alert to unusual activity and report it to the appropriate officials.

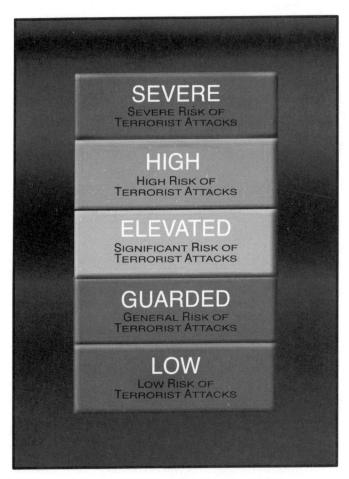

Figure 2. Homeland Security Advisory System.

Yellow: Elevated. An elevated condition is declared when there is a significant risk of terrorist attacks. Suggested activities at the yellow/elevated condition threat level include continuing to be alert for and reporting suspicious activities, conducting a reassessment of your facilities' security, and making any necessary improvements and adjustments.

Orange: High. An orange alert is declared when there is a high risk of terrorist attacks. At this level, continue to be vigilant, and review emergency response plans; management may determine that it is appropriate to further restrict access to facilities and may also consider whether additional security staff is required.

Red: Severe. A red alert reflects a severe risk of terrorist attacks. At this highest risk level, regularly check radio, TV, and newspapers for updated information and instructions from government agencies. Continue to be alert and immediately report unusual activities to authorities. As in a high condition threat, management may decide to further restrict access and may arrange for additional security staff.

In spite of the fact that there are new terrorist threats in our country, most organizations can rest assured that they are not likely to be a direct terrorist target. That does not, however, erase the responsibility to safeguard employees and facilities. Though not a direct terrorist target, an organization may be at risk simply because of its location or who it has as neighbors. While we can never be guaranteed of what the future will bring, answers to a series of questions can provide a general indication of the likelihood that an organization will be the direct or indirect target of a terrorist attack:

- ❑ Is the organization well known locally, nationally, or internationally?
- ❑ Have individuals in your organization been the target of threats, negative publicity, or a great deal of media attention?
- ❑ Are there government agencies or businesses in your building or immediate area who may be a terrorist target?
- ❑ Are you located in a densely populated area?
- ❑ Do tenants of your building or in the area receive negative media exposure?
- ❑ Is there a college, university, or abortion clinic in the area?
- ❑ Is there a large entertainment complex, convention center, stadium, or sports arena nearby?
- ❑ Is your building near a national landmark?

Answering "yes" to one or more these questions indicates a need to train employees how to respond quickly to life-threatening situations resulting from a terrorist attack.

Chemical agents used in biological or chemical terror attacks are generally liquids, often aerosolized, and many have immediate effects; in other cases, effects are delayed for a few hours. Many chemical agents have a unique odor and color. Biological agents differ in that the effects are delayed, often for days. Biological agents have no odor or color and can be in either liquid or powder form.

In spite of the uncertainty surrounding terrorist attacks, staying informed will make your organization better prepared to respond should there be an attack. Stay informed about the types of weapons and tactics used by terrorists. A huge factor in terrorist attacks is striking with little or no warning; be prepared and observe the environment.

A terrorist attack may come in the form of a chemical or biological attack, as a dirty bomb, or it may be of another type yet unknown. Knowing what specific steps to take in response to an act of terrorism is a huge challenge. No one government agency at any level has all the knowledge and capabilities to act in a terrorist attack. The wide range of types of terror attacks makes it impossible to develop one single set of procedures to be used in all situations. In the event of a nuclear, biological, or chemical attack, there are some basic guidelines you can be prepared to follow.

Should your organization be directly or indirectly impacted by a terrorist attack, adopt the same procedures used to respond to other emergencies such as fires or earthquakes. If ordered by officials, facilities and engineering can shut down heating, ventilation, and air conditioning (HVAC) systems to limit the intake of dangerous materials. Restrict access to your building to prevent the spread of any materials. Be prepared to set up decontamination and wash-down stations. Keep a radio tuned to a local radio station to listen for informational updates from officials. This may include sheltering in place, using decontamination and wash-down stations to wash away chemical or biological agents, or being examined by medical professionals.

None of us can see what the future holds, nor can we predict how great a threat terrorism may be in the years ahead or what it may take to prepare and respond. We can stay alert and follow the recommendations of government agencies to lessen the resulting impact of any terrorist attack to the greatest extent possible.

Suspicious Packages and Mail

While no individual or organization is absolutely immune from receiving dangerous mail, evaluating the level of vulnerability is critical in helping you prepare for the possible receipt of a bomb threat or other threatening mail. Answers to the following will provide an indication of your possible level of vulnerability:

❑   Does the organization have offices or outlets in a foreign country?

❑   If so, are you conducting business in countries experiencing civil disturbance or political unrest?

❑ Is yours a highly visible organization whose products, services, or research projects are controversial?

❑ Has your organization recently downsized or reorganized resulting in layoffs?

❑ Is there a history of employee abuse and harassment or workplace violence?

❑ Have any employees made threats to harm fellow employees or to damage the organization?

If the answer to one or more of these questions is "yes," being prepared to handle suspicious mail or packages should move up on the priority list. Additionally, the answers to these questions may be of help in identifying potential sources of threats.

Whatever the vulnerability level, the preferable approach to limiting physical exposure to suspect mailings, including anthrax, is to identify a single point of contact for opening mail away from the general employee population. The mailroom or mail center, previously often unprotected and overlooked in applying safety and security procedures, has now become the focal point of most organizations' defense against suspicious packages and mail.

Develop and conscientiously follow specific screening and inspection procedures for ALL incoming mail and package deliveries. Provide training in identifying and handling suspicious mail for mailroom personnel or others who regularly process mail. Provide appropriate equipment, e.g., gloves for handling all mail, containers for holding and carrying suspicious letters and packages. Establish an isolation area for suspicious packages that is easily accessible and not more than fifty yards distant from the mail screening area. If possible, a covered, outdoor area is preferred, perhaps a loading dock or open storage area. Ensure that everyone in the organization has a complete understanding of the mail-handling process. Based on your organization's level of vulnerability, establishing a policy that any and all packages, envelopes, and other material delivered by any delivery service, courier, or individual must be processed through the mailroom or other central receiving point may be advisable.

For organizations with no mail center and even those where most mail and packages are handled through a central receiving point, all employees should be made familiar with recommended procedures for recognizing a suspicious letter or package and for what to do when a threatening piece of mail is received. The most basic question to ask is simply, "Is there anything about this envelope or package that just doesn't look right?" If so, assume there is a problem and take appropriate action. While not foolproof, the following is based on a list developed by the U.S. Postal Service (USPS) of specific characteristics that should trigger suspicion. (See Figure 3.)

Check the address and return address:

❑ Is the letter or parcel addressed to someone who is no longer with your organization?

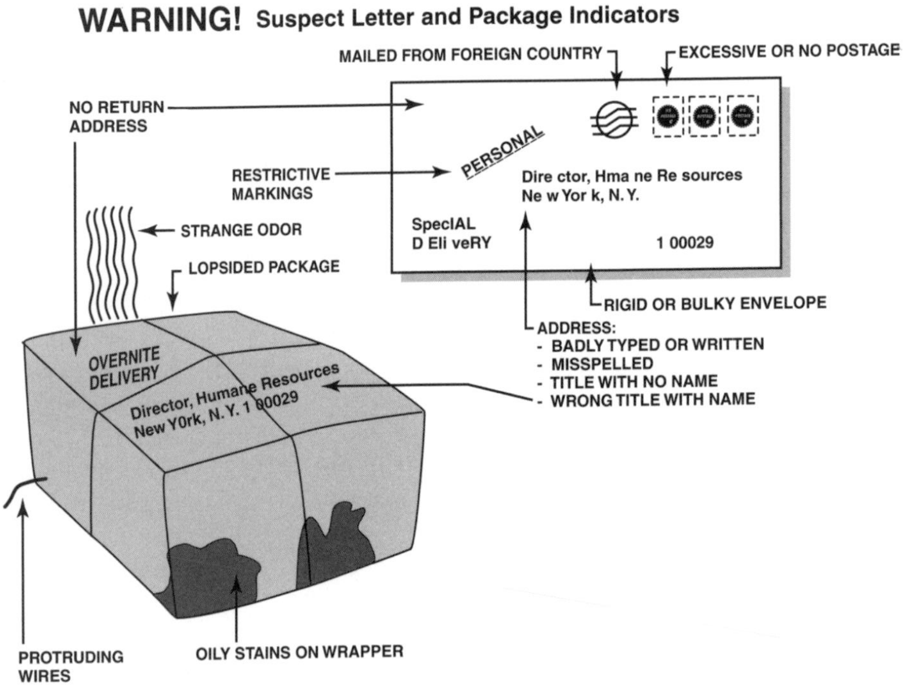

WARNING! Suspect Letter and Package Indicators

Figure 3. Suspicious Letter and Package Indicators.

❑ Is there no return address, or do the return address and the postmark not agree?

❑ Are there misspelled words or is the address badly written or typed?

❑ Has cut-and-paste lettering been used for the address?

❑ Is it addressed to a title only with no name?

❑ Is the package marked "Confidential" or "Personal?"

Look for unusual package characteristics:

❑ Is there a powdery substance on the outside?

❑ Are there strange odors or stains?

❑ Are wires protruding from the package?

❑ Is there an unusual amount of tape or string on the package?

❑ Is the package itself lopsided, oddly shaped, or particularly heavy for its size?

Before calling the police or other officials, an attempt may be made to determine if the person to whom the suspicious package is addressed has any knowledge of the item or its content. There are questions that can be asked of the addressee to help verify the validity of the package:

❑ Are you familiar with the name and address of the sender?

❑ Are you expecting a letter or package from the sender?

❑ Have you purchased or ordered anything from any business that might be located in the city, state, or country where the package originated?

❑ Are you aware of any family members, friends, colleagues, or business acquaintances currently traveling in the area of the package's origin?

If the package has any of the characteristics of an unusual package and/or if the addressee is unable to validate the package, consider the letter or package suspicious and take the following steps.

If you suspect the mail may contain a radiological, biological, or chemical threat, avoid handling it. Do not shake it or drop it. Isolate it as quickly as possible (in a plastic bag or container if possible). Evacuate and cordon off the immediate area. Note all people who have handled or come in contact with the envelope or parcel. As specified by local officials, make the following notifications or request that a supervisor or other person do so: police, fire department or hazardous materials (hazmat) unit, and postal inspectors. Everyone who has touched the item should wash their hands with hot water and soap as soon as possible.

As soon as possible, place all items worn when in contact with the suspect mail in plastic bags and make them available to responding law enforcement units. Shower with soap and water as soon as practical. Unless instructed otherwise by public safety officials, avoid using bleach or other disinfectants. Officials may suggest that you see a physician, or you may opt to do so for your own sense of security.

If you suspect the mail may contain a bomb, evacuate immediately. Call the local fire department or hazmat unit and police and postal inspectors.

The responding officials will assess the threat situation, provide further instructions, and make any additional notifications as required, e.g., FBI, Centers for Disease Control, and local, county, and state health departments. You can assist law enforcement officials by providing information about the package with answers to some questions. When, where, and by what means was the packaged delivered? Who accepted the item? What are the names of all persons who handled the items?

Reference the USPS Web site for more information and a downloadable poster to help employees spot possible dangerous mail.

Sheltering in Place

Sheltering in place is a course of action taken when the risks associated with leaving the building are outweighed by the benefits of staying inside. Sheltering in place is often ordered by public safety officials where there is a release of hazardous materials outside the building. Examples of this are an accident on a nearby highway involving a tanker truck carrying a hazardous material, a train tank car filled with chemicals overturning on a rail line in your area, or a hazardous materials incident at a nearby business such as an oil refinery. Sheltering in place may also be used to avoid possible injuries when there are other dangerous situations such as threats of violence or civil disturbance outside the building.

All employees and visitors should stay inside. Close all doors and windows. Have facilities or engineering shut down the HVAC system to prevent materials from entering the building.

If a shelter-in-place order is issued, remain calm and calm others in your area. Stay at the front desk and encourage everyone to stay where they are and not leave the building until an all-clear order is given. Elevators should not be used. If public safety officials are on site, follow their instructions. To the extent possible, continue with normal work and routines. Listen to local radio stations for information about external conditions and updates on the expected duration of the shelter-in-place order.

If there are people who become overly stressed, obtain assistance for them from the HR or others as designated.

As is the case of most emergency situations, rumors may begin to circulate. Do not pass along information unless you are certain that it is correct and you have been advised to do so.

Again, no two emergency or disaster situations will ever be exactly the same. While one set of procedures cannot fully cover every emergency and disaster, adopting a set of uniform procedures for the threats that are most likely to strike your organization provides everyone with a roadmap for what to do when emergencies and disasters do occur. Having a set of well-thought-out procedures that address the needs of the organization and its employees will guide the organization through any potentially hazardous situation while helping to protect people and property.

DEVELOPING THE PLAN

AS A FRONT DESK PROFESSIONAL YOU MAY, either currently or in the future, be part of the organization's planning group that is charged with developing emergency preparedness and response plans or maintaining, updating, or enhancing existing documents. This involvement offers an excellent opportunity to make an even greater contribution to the organization's capability of safeguarding its people and property.

There is much to be gained through the planning process beyond the development of plans and procedures. There are even some who argue that greater value is gained from the emergency planning process than from the plans that are developed as a result of the process. To quote Dwight D. Eisenhower, the thirty-fourth president of the United States, "Plans are nothing, planning is everything." During the planning process it is likely that you will discover hazards that have not previously been identified, additional mitigation steps that can be taken, a more efficient way to account for employees following an evacuation, or ways to better educate employees about the emergency management program.

That being said, we definitely do need a written plan that outlines the emergency program and details what needs to be done to respond to emergencies and disasters, how it will be done, where it will be done, when it will be done, and by whom it will be done. Our emergency plan is our emergency operating manual, our how-to. Operating without a plan and taking a seat-of-the-pants approach to responding to emergencies and disasters will most assuredly result in an ineffective and possibly catastrophic outcome. Additionally, "Scream and yell and run like hell," is not an adequate plan. The plan needs to be detailed enough to give adequate guidance to people who may be faced by horrific, previously unimaginable situations.

If they are being honest, anyone who has been involved in the development of an emergency preparedness and response plan will tell you that it is neither a trivial nor an inconsequential undertaking. It is critical that the plans and procedures developed result in a successful response. They must be practical and able to be quickly and easily implemented. It can be an intimidating experience, particularly for those who are first-timers.

Because of uncertainties about how to approach developing a plan, it may be tempting to consider taking another organization's document, changing specifics such as names, addresses, and contact information, and calling the plan done. A strong caution—don't do it! Unless your organization is exactly the same type of operation and has exactly the same number of employees doing exactly the same jobs, it won't work. Unless your building is a cookie-cutter version of the other organization's physical plant including building design, infrastructure, life safety systems, grounds, and location, you are asking for trouble.

In regard to emergency management plans, one size does not fit all. Ensure that your plan and procedures take into account the uniqueness of your organization and its people. Duplicating another plan and making some minor changes will not only not work well; it may not work at all, and will possibly result in greater danger, more injuries, and more property damage when a disaster occurs. Your organization's plan must be developed to specifically address all aspects of the organization, including its needs and capabilities.

Developing the plan is a project, and as with any other project, a planned, phased approach breaks the project down into easily managed tasks and helps keep it on track. Here is a sample macro project plan outline for developing an emergency management program that includes an emergency preparedness and response plan.

Basic Project Plan for Developing an Emergency Management Program

Phase I: Project Initiation
Establish the project goal and objectives.
Obtain management's approval and commitment.
Create a project schedule.
Designate planning team members.

Phase II: Hazard Assessment

Identify hazards and risks.

Assess employee needs and skills.

Assess current capabilities.

Develop planning scenarios.

Develop and implement a hazard mitigation program.

Phase III: Plan Development

Develop emergency preparedness and response plan outline.

Establish the emergency response team organization.

Write the initial plan draft.

Designate an emergency response team, including primary members and backups.

Conduct a tabletop exercise to test the draft plan.

Revise the plan.

Circulate the draft plan to management, planning team, ERT members, and others as required for review and comment.

Finalize the plan after reaching a consensus and making revisions as agreed.

Develop ERT checklists.

Obtain the needed supplies and equipment.

Phase IV: Training, Drills, and Exercises

Begin an employee awareness program.

Establish and initiate an ongoing cycle of training, drills, and exercises.

Phase V: Program Maintenance

Assign ongoing ownership of the emergency preparedness and response program.

Establish an ongoing schedule of plan review and updates.

Keep the macro project plan in mind as we explore some of the individual steps in greater detail. If things begin to feel overwhelming, simply refer back to the project plan to help keep the big picture in focus.

The process of developing an emergency preparedness and response program and the related plan begins and ends with the management. In some organizations, management has already realized the value of the program and has initiated the planning process. For others, having an emergency preparedness and response plan is mandated by regulatory agencies or local ordinances. Whatever the case, management must support the idea of emergency planning, provide funding for it, and approve members of the emergency planning committee who dedicate their time to the planning process. When the emergency plan has been completed, it must be approved by management.

In some cases it will be necessary to "sell" the program to management by inform-ing, educating, and creating an awareness of the importance of an emergency management program. If that responsibility falls to you, emphasize the positive aspects of the program, e.g., fulfilling a moral responsibility, possibly reducing insurance claims, being better able to respond to the needs of all employees and other stakeholders when a disaster strikes. Also remember that emergency management is just good business.

If you make a presentation to management to get approval to proceed with an emergency management program, be well prepared. Present the facts and be realistic while avoiding being threatening or taking a gloom-and-doom approach. Use videos and other visual aids if appropriate. Do your homework and address the concerns of management. Be prepared to respond to any specific concerns and questions. Remember that management does not want you to present them with another problem that needs to be solved. Present them with the need for a program together with a solution and an approach for developing the emergency management program. Be concise. It's typical that the higher the position in the organization, the less time you'll have to make your case.

In addition to the requirement that any resources needed to complete the project—including both money and people hours—must be approved by management, it will be necessary to get management-level approval of some items that are typically included in emergency plans. Following are some examples of policy-related issues:

- ❑ Who will have the authority to release employees to go home following an emergency?

- ❑ Will employeese be paid for time not worked as the result of an emergency or disaster?

- ❑ What is the organization's stance on employees making statement to media representatives?

- ❑ Will equipment sign-out procedures be implemented?

It is not logical to expect that any one person can develop a comprehensive emergency plan without help. It takes the combined effort of a group of individuals—a team.

The advantages to taking a team approach to developing your emergency management program are many. A team approach allows for spreading the workload, brings specialized knowledge to the planning process, and provides a broader perspective. As with any undertaking involving more people will shorten the time it takes to complete the project. More people become invested in the process, and the program has greater visibility and stature. If possible, have upper management put all project team appointments in writing and issue a kick-off memo to all employees announcing the project and asking for their support.

A question usually asked at the beginning of the plan development process is, "How long will it take?" This is a difficult question to answer. How many people are working on the project? How much time can each of the people involved devote to the process—

an hour or two a week or 60 per cent of their time? Is this the first emergency preparedness and response plan project any of the team members have participated in, or are there some seasoned veterans in the group? Truthful answers to these questions will help establish a realistic project timeline. And don't get too caught up in getting the project done quickly. Producing an excellent plan is much more important than getting it done in a short amount of time, and rushing things can result in losing out on some of the value of the planning process. Using a team approach can help keep the project moving forward. If there are times when a team member must devote more time to day-to-day responsibilities, it is likely that another person on the team can fill the void by temporarily taking on some additional plan development work.

Should you have the luxury of deciding who will be on the team, here are some of the areas from which you may want to consider having representation: security, facilities, engineering/maintenance, human resources, safety/health, and public relations. Also involve some of the people who will be ERT members. Make the plan and procedures theirs from the beginning by involving them in the plan development process.

There are other areas of the organization that will not necessarily be represented on the planning team, but where you do need to identify a "go to" person for periodic review and approval, to get input on policy and legal issues, or simply to keep the right people in the loop during the planning process. This may include upper management, legal counsel (internal or external), and auditors (internal and/or external). If your organization has bargaining units, determine whether it is appropriate to have union representation in the planning group.

There is no such thing as perfect foresight, and no emergency preparedness and response plan can predict every eventuality. The purpose of the planning process is to produce a realistic assessment of the hazards your organization faces, and to develop a program including emergency response procedures that will deal with those hazards. Those same emergency responses will also enable you to deal effectively with other hazards you have not anticipated.

To identify your organization's most likely disasters and emergencies, conduct a hazard assessment:

- ❑ What are the disasters that the organization has faced in the past?
- ❑ What do public safety officials see as the most likely events to impact your organization?
- ❑ What do your internal experts—security, facilities, HR, safety—see as the greatest threats?
- ❑ If they occur, how will these threats impact people, facilities, and the organization's ability to continue operations?
- ❑ What is currently in place to address and respond to the identified threats?

This information is key to identifying needed mitigation measures and making certain that a realistic approach will be taken to develop plans and procedures for the emergencies and disasters that are most likely to occur.

The groundwork is laid and it's time to begin the plan development process. First, a few things about the actual plan document. Binders work well for plan documents; individual pages or sections can be revised without creating a need to reprint and bind the entire document each time the plan is updated. Each and every page of the document should be numbered and should include the date of the latest revision. A revision number may also be included. Develop a detailed table of contents and use tabs printed with section titles to make the document more user-friendly.

Here are some basics for making your plan more useful. First and foremost, write the plan as though you and other people involved in developing it will leave the organization immediately after the plan is completed and will not be there to interpret the plan or fill in any blanks when the plan is activated.

Keep it as short and simple as possible. Give the level of detail only to the degree absolutely necessary, and not one word more. With regard to plan documents, volume does not equal excellence. Use plain and clear language. Write for the readers, using terms and phrases familiar to everyone. Avoid full pages of text. Bullets and short paragraphs are easier to read quickly. Diagrams, charts, and pictures are even better. Use appendices if it is necessary to include detailed or highly technical information. Remember to use attachments for forms and all items that will be updated frequently.

Additional tips: In the body of the plan refer to people by title or position rather than by name to avoid having to make frequent plan revisions. Include individuals' names and specific contact information in plan attachments. Necessary notifications are often overlooked and omitted from the plan. Think through and identify all people, organizations, and other entities who must be contacted when an emergency occurs and those to be notified once the emergency has passed. If your organization has staff technical writers, they can often help pare down the number of pages in a plan document with some expert editing.

Your organization may have other disaster-related programs and/or plans, including business recovery (BRP), disaster recovery (DRP), business continuity (BCP), crisis communications (CCP), continuity of operations (COOP), or continuity of government (COG) plans. These programs and their related plans primarily address how the organization's operations will be resumed or continued following a disaster event. Check with the person(s) who maintains these plans to determine if integration and coordination of the emergency preparedness and response program and these other programs is necessary.

Consider using this approach for writing the plan document. The planning group begins the process by developing a detailed outline of the plan. You may want to use the outline below as a model and starting point, customizing it as necessary. At the risk of repeating myself, I am going to say that it is extremely unlikely that this outline will be perfect as is for your organization. Adjust and tailor it as necessary to meet your needs.

Emergency Preparedness and Response Plan Outline

Plan Distribution (List all holders of the plan document; also consider numbering each copy of the plan for control and to be certain that all holders of the plan get all revisions.)

Record of Plan Changes (List each change in the plan; include the date the change was made, the section/pages revised, and the name or initials of the person who made the changes.)

Table of Contents (Make it detailed for ease of use.)

Foreword (This is the endorsement of the plan, signed by a representative of upper management.)

Glossary (Include the definitions of words and acronyms that are emergency-management specific or that may not be familiar to all employees.)

Section

I. Introduction
   A. Purpose
   B. Objectives
   C. Emergency management policy
   D. Workplace violence policy
   E. Authorities and references
   F. How to use this plan

II. Emergency Preparedness Program
   A. Building preparedness
   B. Employee preparedness
   C. Home and family preparedness
   D. Assistance to disabled individuals
   E. Posting of emergency procedures
   F. Emergency procedures review and update

G. Fire prevention program

H. Preparedness measures for natural disasters (hurricane, tornado, snowstorm, earthquake, tsunami, etc.)

I. Emergency supplies and equipment

J. Training, drills, and exercises

III. Emergency Response Program

    A. Emergency response team organization

    B. Alert and warning systems

    C. Security of critical facilities

    D. Off-hours occurrence

    E. Preparing for evacuation

    F. Outdoor assembly area

    G. Evacuation

    H. Accounting for personnel

    I. First-aid care

IV. Emergency Procedures

    A. Medical emergencies

    B. Fire

    C. Natural disasters (flood, hurricane, tornado, snowstorm, earthquake, tsunami, etc.)

    D. Building evacuation

    E. Power outage

    F. Bomb threat

    G. Workplace violence incident

    H. Terrorist attack

    I. Suspicious mail or package

    J. Sheltering in place

V. Security

    A. Unusual occurrences

    B. Access controls

    C. Property removal

    D. Security notification procedures

Attachments

    A. Emergency contact numbers

    B. Emergency procedures

    C. Life safety system features

    D Outdoor assembly area map

    E. Emergency management program committee membership

    F. Emergency response team members

    G. Emergency response team checklists

    H. Emergency supplies and equipment inventory

    I. First-aid and CPR-trained personnel

    J. Defibrillator instructions

    K. Fire-extinguisher-trained personnel

    L. Floor plans (showing evacuation routes and location of fire pulls, fire extinguishers, first aid supplies, emergency equipment, etc.)

    M. Emergency telephones

    N. Emergency generator information

    O. Fire extinguisher instructions

    P. Assisting disabled persons

    Q. Bomb threat checklist

    R. Property removal form

    S. Instructions for remote 800 lines

    T. Visitor emergency procedures

Once the team reaches agreement that the outline represents a plan document that will fully meet your organization's emergency management needs, assign responsibility for writing specific sections of the plan to each person on the team. To the extent possible, give people sections that are a good fit with their expertise and experience. Pull the completed individual sections together, edit for consistency, and fill in any gaps. You now have the first draft. Have all team members review the initial draft and submit comments. After incorporating agreed-upon changes into the plan, create a second draft. Next, conduct a tabletop exercise to test the plan and identify deficiencies and inaccuracies, and make all necessary corrections. After getting management's approval, finalize and distribute the plan.

It is not necessary to distribute the full plan document to all employees. Typically, upper management, department managers, and ERT members have individual copies of the full plan. A printed copy of the emergency procedures, perhaps in a checklist format, is distributed to all employees.

A word of caution: An emergency management planning project has no true "end." Establishing the emergency management program and creating the emergency preparedness and response plan is not a check-the-box process. Just when it feels as though you are reaching the end, you realize you are only beginning.

This is an ongoing process. It is essential to assign ongoing program ownership without which the project will quickly deteriorate once the initial planning process is concluded. The program owner, perhaps with a title similar to emergency management coordinator, is often the same person who manages the planning process, but ownership may be assigned to a different person once the planning process has been completed. While the planning process is not easy, the really challenging task is keeping the plan current in the face of change. Without permanent ownership, it is most likely that essential steps such as plan reviews and updates and ongoing training and testing will not happen. Within six months to a year, all the good work will have been for naught as your organization and its operation change, and the viability of your program fades into the sunset.

An essential component of your emergency management program, plan documents are not static and are never complete. Like people, they should grow, mature, and get better with time and experience. Conduct a formal audit of the entire plan no less than annually.

There are multiple triggers for updating plans and procedures. Some examples of the things that will necessitate plan updates are changes in the physical plant, building remodeling or restacking, or major equipment changes; changes in hazard and vulnerability information, e.g., a fireworks company moves into your business park; changes in the organization's policies; changes in regulations or local ordinances; organizational changes, e.g., mergersor reorganizations; general changes in personnel (increasing or decreasing numbers) and specific personnel changes, e.g., ERT personnel; and changes in contact information (likely to be the change category you will most often experience). The other major plan change trigger is experience gained from drills, exercises, and actual emergencies and disasters. It is almost a certainty that each time the plan is put into play, whether for a staged exercise or for an actual event, needed improvements and changes will be identified.

Successful response to emergencies and disasters results not from luck or from fate but from an analysis of possible situations and the development and proper testing and execution of plans and procedures. As a result of an ever-changing environment, unforeseen circumstances, and other variables, plans will not always be 100 percent successful as they are originally developed. Plans do, however, greatly increase the chance for a more efficient and successful response to an emergency or disaster. . .for ensuring the safety and security of everyone in your organization.

CHAPTER 6

BEYOND THE MANUAL—THE HUMAN COMPONENT

IN EARLIER CHAPTERS WE EXPLORED MANY FACETS OF SAFETY, security, and emergency management. Life safety systems, procedures, plans, equipment and supplies, an emergency organization, and training and exercises—each plays an integral part in protecting people and property. Removing any of these would lessen the organization's ability to successfully respond to emergencies and disasters.

Yet beyond those factors, there are other elements that come into play. Each of these, in a very different way, directly involves people, and it is people that matter most.

In this chapter we will look at the importance of dealing with the stress, and sometimes the trauma, people experience following a disaster and some ways to avoid or alleviate the negative effects of post-disaster emotional stress. In addition to the preparations we make at work, we also need to prepare our homes and families for future disasters. Visitors with special needs who are in your front desk area may require additional assistance in an emergency. This is particularly true when it is necessary to evacuate the building. Some ways of providing the necessary help are outlined.

And let's not overlook another key human element—you, the front desk professional, the person. Your communication and people skills, your concern about the well-being of colleagues and visitors to your organization, your insights, and at times even your intuition all come into play. We'll look at the importance of the human factor you bring to your front desk safety, security, and emergency response role.

Meeting Special Needs

Beyond the basics of mitigation, preparedness, response, and recovery, it is important to be prepared to address several special needs that arise when a disaster occurs. In particular it is important to be prepared to lessen the inevitable stress that occurs when disasters happen and that we can respond to the needs of those with disabilities,

Disaster-Related Stress

Disasters don't happen just to organizations and buildings; their greatest impact is on people. When a disaster event impacts an organization, varying levels of stress are pervasive among the employees who work there. Natural disasters that result in widespread destruction and loss of life, any event that results in serious injuries or the death of a loved one, friend, or coworker, and serious work-related accidents are particularly traumatic. Some disasters, such as a terrorist attack, result in a threat that continues over a long period of time and may create ongoing insecurity and fear, making it more difficult for some people to function well in their day-to-day lives.

Experiencing stress following a shocking event or disaster, either as a victim or as a witness, is normal. Disasters are often accompanied by a frightening array of sensory stimuli, both sights and sounds. There is a feeling of loss of control over one's physical world and a concern for one's own physical safety and that of loved ones, friends, and colleagues. The resulting stress is often exacerbated by a fear that the event will happen again.

When a disaster occurs, particularly a natural disaster that impacts the entire community and not just the workplace, dedicated employees have responsibilities to their homes and families, perhaps both children and older relatives, in addition to their daily and emergency responsibilities at work. This need to "serve two masters" by fulfilling both work and home responsibilities creates a role conflict and an accompanying additional layer of stress.

Each person handles disaster-related stress differently. For some the stress is apparent immediately and may be long term. Signs of this immediate stress include extreme fear, disbelief, and shock. People may have a difficult time making basic decisions or even refuse to leave a dangerous area. For others the stress may only become apparent long after the actual disaster occurs. Some of the signs of this stress may include sleeplessness, appetite changes, frequent headaches, mental confusion, nightmares, changes in behavior, or mood changes such as depression, anxiety, or anger. It is interesting to note that, in spite of what is commonly believed to be true, past disasters have shown that while people may experience excessive alarm or fear, panic is rare.

There are some steps that can be taken immediately and in the longer term to provide assistance. First and foremost, calm and reassure those exhibiting signs of stress. Show that you care while accepting the person's concerns as real. Be positive. Often the best emotional first aid you can provide is simply to encourage the person to talk. People don't necessarily expect you to make the situation go away or want you to solve their problems—they just want someone to listen.

Providing people with adequate information about what is happening, offering reassurance that the threat of death or serious injury has passed, and letting them know that they will be able to leave the building all help calm people and prevent trauma. Just knowing that there is leadership and direction leads to lowered stress levels. Establishing communication channels and keeping employees accurately informed about the situation is also important in lowering their stress levels. Human beings do not like to operate in an information vacuum.

In those cases where the stress level continues to build or a person does experience a panic attack, separate the overly stressed person from other employees and visitors by asking someone to take them to a quiet office and stay with them while you summon help. Bringing into play human resource professions can help lower the level of stress. As specified in your plan, contact security or HR for assistance.

It is important to know and accept your own limitations. You cannot be all things to all people. While most people will be able to recover on their own, some victims and people witnessing disasters will need additional attention from a professional therapist to normalize their feelings and find effective ways of coping with ongoing stress. In those cases, recommend that the person seek help.

Again, if your organization has an employee assistance program, it is an excellent source of aid. The organization may opt to immediately provide group and/or one-on-one counseling following an emergency, particularly in cases where lives have been lost or serious injuries have occurred. If not, refer those whose disaster-related stress is severe or those whose stress symptoms continue to HR or directly to the employee assistance program or encourage them to seek help through other channels.

Assisting the Disabled

The Americans with Disabilities Act (ADA) defines a disabled person as anyone who has a physical or mental impairment that substantially limits one or more major life activities. ADA requires that every employer provide every employee with the same level of safety as everyone else. At the time of an emergency, particularly one necessitating building evacuation, disabled persons may require help to get out of the building safely. Others, for example an employee who has broken a leg while skiing, may require special assistance on a temporary basis.

People with disabilities can best determine what form of evacuation assistance may be needed. Consequently, pre-assigned coworker "buddies" should confer with the employee with a disability *before* an emergency occurs to determine the type of assistance required. Since coworker "buddies" may be the eyes and ears of sight and hearing impaired employees, it is important that the buddies keep the person they are assisting informed of what is happening during an emergency.

If there are people with special needs in the front desk area at the time of an emergency, there are some basic things you can do to provide the necessary assistance.

Mobility Impairment

Many persons with mobility impairments can walk with assistance, even under emergency conditions. Others may need to be carried to a safe location. The individual should be consulted regarding the best method for providing assistance, particularly those who are in a wheelchair. This should be done before an emergency occurs.

When you talk with a mobility-impaired person, talk with the person at eye level. Ask the person how you can best help, then explain what you are going to do before each step you take. If an evacuation device is available (e.g., evacuation chair) and you are moving a wheelchair-dependent person to the device, again ask how best to lift and move them if they are not able to raise themselves. Remember to set the brakes on the wheelchair before moving the person from the chair. Check with local public safety officials to discuss their procedures for evacuating mobility-impaired people.

Visual Impairment

Visually impaired persons are usually very familiar with and comfortable in their usual surroundings. In some cases, they may actually be able to assist sighted people in situations where there is little or no light. Employees who are visually impaired and use a white cane should be encouraged to keep an extra cane available at the workplace. Again, always let the person choose what, if any, help is needed.

To assist visually impaired people, before an emergency occurs, read and describe any written or visual emergency procedures. When giving emergency instructions, identify yourself and maintain physical contact such as a hand on the arm or shoulder. Do provide verbal instructions and physical assistance such as letting the person take your arm while walking. Always let the person choose what help is needed. When giving directions, use "clock face" descriptions such as "The emergency exit is to the left at 10:00." Inform the person of any approaching barriers or obstacles and describe doorways, stairs, slanted floors, or narrow spaces. Do not raise your voice when speaking. Remember that a person who is visually impaired most likely has excellent hearing.

Hearing Impairment

Many hearing-impaired persons are able to read lips very well and can understand sign language. Those who use a hearing aid should be encouraged to keep extra batteries at the workplace. Again, let the person advise you as to the best way to provide them with assistance.

Provide a person who is hearing impaired with written or visual, not verbal, emergency procedures. Use paper and a pen or pencil to write messages. Wave or tap the person gently on the shoulder or hand to attract their attention. Directly face the person and speak slowly and distinctly.

Additional information on emergency procedures for employees with disabilities is available at no cost from the United States Fire Administration and FEMA. "Emergency Procedures for Employees with Disabilities in Office Occupancies" provides useful information covering the safe evacuation of people who might need special assistance in emergency situations and details types of equipment that provide safe egress. Available in English, Spanish, Braille, and audio cassette, the publication can be ordered from the FEMA Website, USFA On-Line Publications Section.

It's All About You

Your building is equipped with sophisticated life safety and security systems. A practical, well-written plan is in place that contains easy-to-follow procedures for the emergencies and disasters that may impact your organization. The procedures have been communicated throughout the organization, and a training program is in place. Still, there is another element that is often taken for granted and that greatly impacts the success of the efforts to prevent and respond to emergency situations. . .the human factor.

Heeding Danger Signals

Awareness of what is happening is no less important than the security systems.

A big component of this awareness is the seemingly simply process of paying attention to what is being said and noticing the actions of those in the front desk area. Make sure that a lack of attention doesn't prevent you from picking up on any danger signals that may be forecasting impending danger.

Use your senses by watching and listening. Start by tuning in to what's happening in the front desk area. Listening and observing purposefully will help you read people. The majority of what people communicate is not through words. Watch people's body language and facial expressions. Does the person you're talking with have their arms crossed? Are they facing you or avoiding looking at you? "Listen" for any unspoken messages. Be aware of the intent of the message as well as the content of the words. Notice if you are feeling that a person is not telling you everything. Conversely, is the person talking too much or asking too many questions?

Sharpen your listening skills. It will help you avoid having to say, "I had no idea that. . ." or finding something happened "without warning." Recovering from a crisis requires far more time and effort than would have been required if we had just listened to all of both the spoken and unspoken clues that were there from the beginning.

To be a better listener, clear your mind. Make eye contact when you're talking with someone. Doing so tells the other person you're paying attention to and value what they're saying. Watch the eyes; hear the tone; pay attention to expressions. Listen to all the words being said before you begin making assumptions, forming conclusions, and planning your response. The more you practice picking up on the unspoken messages people deliver, the more skillful you will be at picking up any red flags that are waved in front of you.

Beyond the more commonly thought of ways to be aware of possible danger signals, there is one more important component to include—your intuition.

Heeding Your Intuition

Have you ever noticed a funny feeling in your stomach or your neck? Have you ever felt yourself becoming increasingly uncomfortable with a situation at the front desk or when you see a person coming through the entry to the building? Have you ever had a strong feeling that something was going to happen before it actually did? If so, what you experienced was a "gut feeling"—you were using your intuition.

Intuition, the ability to know something directly without going through an analytical process, is a way of understanding without explanations or without consciously seeing a great deal of evidence. When we hear that little voice of experience, that feeling in the pit of our stomach, we often tell ourselves, "It's just my imagination," or "It's probably really nothing." That denial we were hearing was our logical mind asserting itself, pushing the intuitive thoughts aside. And have you ever wished later that you had listened and paid attention to your initial feeling?

While intuition is not a substitute for logical or analytical thinking, hard work, factual knowledge, or formal education, intuitive messages should be brought into the decision-making process, not dismissed out of hand, particularly when the message is strong or does not go away.

One thing intuition can help us do is to head off and avoid disasters. Listen to your gut when you just "don't feel right" around someone who seems polite, is professionally dressed, and cordial, or when you encounter someone who is somewhere in your building where they should not be, or when someone waiting near the front desk makes you extremely uncomfortable. Don't ignore your intuition if the hair goes up on the back of your neck when you hear a noise as you're heading for your car at the end of a long work day, or when the thought of someone you saw behaving strangely near the entrance to your building keeps returning throughout the day. Beware of succumbing to a "give it time and see what happens next" syndrome. If you are having strong feelings about the situation, odds are there's something behind those feelings. Take the time to assess what you've seen and heard and what you feel, and take appropriate action.

When your intuition creates worry, alarm, or fear, trust that intuition. That gut feeling is quite likely sending you messages that are in the best interests of you and your organization. If you feel it's necessary to act immediately, do what it takes to protect the safety and security of yourself and others. If you are not yet ready to act, get a second opinion or seek help and then decide what steps are appropriate.

And what if that gut feeling was wrong and there was no danger? What if it was "really nothing"? Given the choice of ignoring your intuition and as a result failing to prevent harm to yourself and others, or acting on a gut feeling that wasn't right and perhaps experiencing some embarrassment, what is your choice? Safety and security are vitally important; the risk of being wrong may pale in comparison.

Keep things in balance. Act on your intuition after further exploration. Our best decisions are those that combine intuitive thoughts with the facts and the knowledge gained through our education and real world experiences. Intuition does not replace good judgment; it adds to and enhances it.

One of your best single sources for protecting yourself, your colleagues and visitors, and your company's interests is perhaps your intuition. We are incredibly good at foreseeing other people's behavior and picking up on hidden danger signals, yet we often ignore what we intuitively know and foresee. It is important to remember that intuitive thoughts and gut feelings are always in response to something. Trust your intuition. Ignoring the messages we get from our intuition may be one of the biggest obstacles to preventing potential emergencies and disasters.

Parting Thoughts

Most organizations know that taking the steps necessary to address safety and security issues is the right thing to do. What actually drives the decision to develop and implement an emergency management program may be the stick—the necessity of meeting regulatory requirements or local safety ordinances to avoid the possibility of related fines and penalties—or the carrot—a desire to protect all employees, other people, and the organization's physical assets. Whatever the impetus, it is important to think of emergency management planning as an investment in the company, not just another cost of doing business. Yet there are a multitude of reasons why organizations fail to institute continuing efforts to mitigate against potential hazards and make preparations to respond to security and safety threats.

The ability to forget the unpleasant is both a blessing and a curse. We don't like to think about or dwell on unpleasant things so we try to avoid unpleasant memories. This is both good—it allows us to move forward after tragic events—and bad—we lose opportunities to learn from experience and prepare for the future.

Another factor that impedes emergency management planning is the issue of the attention cycle. As it relates to disasters, it looks something like this:

Only a few people in the organization pay attention to safety and security issues and the need for developing and maintaining an emergency preparedness and response program. The rest play ostrich and bury their heads in the sand, either denying or ignoring the fact that danger and vulnerability even exist.

Then a disaster happens. It could be a disaster of such magnitude that it cannot be ignored. Or perhaps it is an emergency that occurs at your location, or maybe in your geographic area, or to an organization similar to yours. That is when we see alarmed discovery, a realization that vulnerabilities exist, that disasters actually do happen. This alarmed discovery is most often accompanied by varying levels of frenzy and/or chaos and impassioned calls to "Do something!" Committees are formed, meetings are held, and grandiose projections are developed.

And time passes. The initial memories of the disaster begin to dim, and there is a return to quiescence. This is accompanied by a realization that the actions required to establish a first-rate emergency management program will require resources (financial and people). Priorities shift. It's time to develop next year's budget, roll out a new product, schedule vacations, conduct performance evaluations, or meet growing requirements for regulatory reporting. All this leads to a general loss of attention and focus by most. Those who were assigned to emergency planning duties are reassigned, and safety and security budgets shrink. Sooner or later, you're back at square one. Again, only a few people are paying attention to safety, security, and disaster preparedness planning, and their pleas for participation, support, and funding fall on deaf ears.

To avoid having your organization risk being unprepared for the next inevitable emergency or major disaster, whatever it may be, it is critical that everyone be involved. If there is no existing emergency management program, work with others in your organization to gain senior management's support of and *commitment* to such a program. This will help ensure that the resources are available to develop and, even more importantly, maintain a comprehensive program to meet the safety and security needs of the organization. Making emergency management as much a part of the organization's culture and day-to-day operations as are accounting, human resources, and marketing can only happen with this level of involvement and support.

Stay safe.

GLOSSARY

9-1-1

The telephone call-in number of a public safety program in Canada and the United States. Anyone calling this number is matched with communications answering and/or dispatch centers for emergency response agencies such as law enforcement, fire and rescue, and emergency medical services.

activation

The implementation of emergency response plans, procedures, and personnel in response to an emergency or disaster.

Americans with Disabilities Act (ADA)

Enacted by the U.S. Senate and House of Representatives in 1990 and enforced by the U.S. Department of Justice to establish a clear and comprehensive prohibition of discrimination on the basis of disability.

American Red Cross (ARC)

Not-for-profit organization that provides disaster and emergency relief and training in lifesaving skills such as CPR and first aid, collects and distributes half the nation's blood supply, and distributes publications on emergency preparation and response.

anthrax

Bacterial disease caused by *Bacillus anthracis*. Occurs in domesticated and wild animals. Infection is introduced through scratches or abrasions of the skin, wounds, inhalation of spores, eating insufficiently cooked infected meat, or from flies. Anthrax spores may remain viable for many years in soil and water.

bioterrorism

The unlawful use, or threatened use, of biological agents (microorganisms or toxins) to produce death or disease and/or to promote or spread fear or intimidation upon an individual, a specific group, or the population as a whole for religious, political, ideological, financial, or personal purposes.

buddy system

The system of assigning the appropriate individual(s) to assist those with special needs during an evacuation.

checklist

A list of specific step-by-step actions taken in response to a particular emergency event or situation.

Closed Circuit Television (CCTV)

Cameras strategically placed in a building or set of buildings and directly linked to monitoring and recording systems typically used for security and safety purposes. CCTV cameras have no public broadcasting capabilities.

crisis

An event that threatens life, property, or business operations beyond acceptable losses unless controlled. From Webster's: "a turning point for better or worse, a crucial time, a decisive moment."

damage assessment

Process of assessing damage following a disaster to determine what equipment, records, facilities, etc., can be salvaged or restored and what must be replaced.

disaster

A major emergency. A destructive or disruptive event, usually sudden, beyond the capabilities of the response organizations where it has occurred. Typically threatens lives and safety and brings great damage, loss, or destruction.

drill (also referred to as exercise)

An activity designed to promote emergency management preparedness; a process to evaluate emergency operations planning, procedures, or facilities; also means of providing training for personnel assigned as members of emergency response teams and the general employee population.

emergency

A condition of disaster or of extreme peril to the safety of persons and property. An unplanned event that can cause deaths or significant injuries or physical or environmental damage. Emergencies can be large or small.

emergency management

The dynamic process of preparing for, mitigating, responding to, and recovering from an emergency.

emergency management program

Program to prepare an organization to mitigate against, prepare for, respond to, and recover from any event that threatens lives, property, or business operations. An emergency management program includes planning, training, conducting drills, testing equipment, and coordinating activities.

emergency preparedness

Discipline to ensure an organization's or community's readiness to respond to an emergency in a coordinated, timely, and effective manner.

emergency response team (ERT)

Teams of designated employees organized, trained, and equipped to respond to emergencies occurring at the organization's facilities by providing assistance to employees and visitors and, as required, directing building evacuation.

exercise

An activity designed to provide training for personnel assigned to emergency response duties and to evaluate emergency plans and procedures.

Federal Emergency Management Agency (FEMA)

Federal government agency with more than 2,600 full-time employees responsible for supporting disaster preparedness, response, and recovery efforts by state and local government agencies.

hazard

Any source of damage or element of risk. There are three types of hazards: natural, technological, and incited (human). See threat.

hazard assessment (also referred to as risk assessment)

Identification of the most probable threats and the analysis of the related consequences. Evaluation of existing physical and environmental security and controls, and assessing existing adequacy relative to the potential threats to the organization.

hazardous material (Hazmat) incident

Stationary: Any uncontrolled release of material capable of posing a risk to health, safety, and property. Areas at risk include facilities that produce, process, or store hazardous material as well as all sites that treat, store, and dispose of hazardous material.

Transportation: Any spill during transport of material that is potentially a risk to health and safety.

Homeland Security, Department of

The department of the U.S. federal government that, in the event of a terrorist attack, natural disaster, or other large-scale emergency, has primary responsibility for ensuring that emergency response professionals are prepared for any situation. Provides a coordinated, comprehensive federal response to any large-scale crisis. Includes FEMA.

infrastructure

A general term including all systems for storing, treating, and distributing fuel, communications, water, sewage, and electricity.

mitigation

Pre-event planning and long-term actions taken to lessen the effects of potential disasters; actions taken in advance of a destructive or disruptive event to reduce, avoid, or protect against loss of life or property from a hazardous event.

National Oceanic and Atmospheric Administration (NOAA)

A division of the Department of Commerce that is engaged in scientific and technical research on oceans and the atmosphere; topics of focus include climate and weather.

OSHA (Occupational Safety and Health Administration)

A division of the Department of Labor that sets and enforces occupational health and safety rules.

preparedness

Actions taken before a destructive or disruptive event to lessen its impacts (i.e., to save lives and minimize damage).

public relations representative, press representative, or public information officer (PIO)

An individual responsible for all media contact on behalf of the organization and to whom all media requests for information are referred following an emergency or disaster. Prepares press releases, conducts media briefings, and arranges for press conferences.

response

Immediate actions taken during and immediately following a destructive or disruptive event to reduce its impacts or to stop its effects.

safety coordinator or health and safety coordinator

Designated employee assigned to monitor and correct unsafe conditions to assure safety of personnel.

scenario

A brief narrative describing a destructive or disruptive event. Beginning with a believable event, a scenario identifies the setting, describes the emergency, and outlines its impacts. Used as a starting point for tabletop or functional exercises, scenarios can also be used as a basis for developing emergency response plans and procedures.

terrorism

Systematic use of terror, force, or unpredictable violence against property, governments, or individuals to attain a political objective.

threat

Any event that will deny your organization the use of your normal work area or the connectivity to that area. See hazard. An expression of intention to hurt, destroy, or cause harm to people or property.

U.S. Fire Administration

Entity of the Department of Homeland Security and the Federal Emergency Management Agency. Mission is to reduce life and economic losses due to fire and related emergencies, through leadership, advocacy, coordination and support.

weapons of mass destruction (WMD)

Typically refers to nuclear, chemical (toxic or poisonous chemical or gas), and biological (disease organism such as smallpox, botulism, or anthrax) weapons designed or intended to cause death or serious injury to large numbers of people. The target is generally civilians or noncombatants.

READINESS ASSESSMENT

Use the following to conduct a basic assessment of your organization's current level of safety and security preparedness. For each statement, circle a score from 1 to 5, *5 being the highest score, 1 the lowest* (1 = nothing currently in place; 3 = exists but needs improvement; 5 = fully meets needs). Total your score for each of the four sections and enter the score on the final page of this assessment to calculate your overall score.

	Low				High
1. Facilities and Life Safety Systems					
Our building is equipped with life safety systems including: emergency lighting, a fire suppression system, fire extinguishers, fire alarm system.	1	2	3	4	5
A system is in place to ensure regular (no less than annual) inspections to identify and correct structural and nonstructural hazards.	1	2	3	4	5
We have organized and trained emergency response teams (ERTs).	1	2	3	4	5

Our organization maintains and regularly inventories and updates emergency supplies and equipment.	1	2	3	4	5
Our organization has a written emergency preparedness and response plan that includes procedures to follow when disasters occur.	1	2	3	4	5
A printed copy of the organization's emergency procedures is provided to each employee.	1	2	3	4	5
Emergency procedures are posted in all public areas of the building(s), e.g., reception area, conference rooms, coffee rooms.	1	2	3	4	5

Total Score for Section 1 ___

2. Security

We have physical security measures in place that include access control of employees and visitors.	1	2	3	4	5
A policy that no doors are to be propped open at any time is strictly enforced.	1	2	3	4	5
Our organization has a policy that requires employees to sign out and sign back in any equipment that is taken from the building.	1	2	3	4	5
A policy has been adopted and is enforced that requires all visitors to sign in and be escorted at all times.	1	2	3	4	5
Our organization has established and enforces a zero tolerance policy that requires that any and all violent actions or threats of violence will be reported.	1	2	3	4	5
We have security guards on site during business hours.	1	2	3	4	5
An exterior lighting system provides sufficient lighting for walkways and parking areas.	1	2	3	4	5

Total Score for Section 2 ___

3. Training

Our organization provides new employee orientation and refresher training for all employees in life safety and security procedures (e.g., evacuation, bomb threats, medical emergencies).	1	2	3	4	5

Training in CPR, first aid, and use of fire extinguishers is made available to employees.	1	2	3	4	5

Training in CPR, first aid, and use of fire extinguishers
is made available to employees.   1   2   3   4   5

We have an established schedule of emergency
training, drills, and exercise   1   2   3   4   5

A full evacuation drill is conducted twice annually.   1   2   3   4   5

Mailroom staff are trained and equipped to handle
suspicious mail and packages.   1   2   3   4   5

Front desk personnel have been trained to
recognize and handle suspicious letters and packages.   1   2   3   4   5

Safety, security, and emergency updates and briefings
are a regular part of departmental staff meetings.   1   2   3   4   5

Total Score for Section 3 ___

4. Front Desk Preparedness

The front desk is positioned and the front desk area is
arranged to provide an unobstructed view of doorways
and of those coming and going.   1   2   3   4   5

Emergency contact numbers (public safety agencies,
internal security staff) are readily available at the front
desk and reviewed for accuracy not less than quarterly.   1   2   3   4   5

A flashlight and extra batteries are kept at the front desk.   1   2   3   4   5

A portable radio and extra batteries are kept at the front
desk.   1   2   3   4   5

Front desk personnel have been trained to handle
telephone bomb threats.   1   2   3   4   5

There is a mechanism in place at the front desk,
e.g., panic button, silent alarm, for covertly calling for
help in a threatening or potentially dangerous situation.   1   2   3   4   5

Code words have been established to alert security
or other personnel should there be a need for
immediate assistance at the front desk.   1   2   3   4   5

Total Score for Section 4 ___

Transfer the total score from each section.

	Actual Total/Possible Total
1. Facilities and Life Safety Systems	_____ /35
2. Security	_____ /35
3. Training	_____ /35
4. Front Desk Preparedness	_____ /35
OVERALL SCORE	_____ /140

After completing this assessment, list some of the areas needing the most improvement. Identify items that could be addressed relatively quickly and easily to increase your organization's level of preparedness.

_____

_____

_____

_____

Discuss the results of this assessment and your suggestions for improvements with others in your organization who are involved in safety and security planning or who may support developing improved or new plans and procedures.

_____

EMERGENCY PROCEDURES CHECKLISTS

EMERGENCY CONTACT NUMBERS

Fire, Law Enforcement, Medical Emergency   9-1-1

Nearest First-aid/CPR-Trained Employee(s)

_____

Building security _____

Facilities/Engineering _____

Ambulance service _____

Nearest hospital/urgent care facility _____

Postal inspector _____

Local FBI office _____

Alarm company _____

Floor/area warden _____

Assembly area _____

Assembly area coordinator _____

Local radio station _____

Calling 9-1-1

- ❑ Never assume someone else called.
- ❑ Stay calm.
- ❑ Speak slowly and clearly.
- ❑ Provide the following information:
  - ❑ Your name
  - ❑ Type of emergency—fire, injury, etc.
  - ❑ Location—street address, cross street
  - ❑ Name of organization
  - ❑ Exact location in building—floor, room number
  - ❑ Your phone number including extension
- ❑ Have someone meet responders at building entrance.
- ❑ Arrange to have an elevator held.
- ❑ Have someone meet the elevator at the destination floor.
- ❑ If not in danger, stay on the line until told to hang up.

Medical Emergency or Injury

- ❑ Assess the situation.
- ❑ Get help—call out for:
  - ❑ A first-aid/CPR-trained person
  - ❑ Someone to phone 9-1-1
  - ❑ Someone to notify security
  - ❑ Someone to meet responding fire/emergency medical personnel
- ❑ Be calm and reassuring.
- ❑ Keep bystanders away.
- ❑ Do not move the person unless:
  - ❑ The victim is in imminent danger.
  - ❑ Assistance cannot be provided without moving the person.
- ❑ Keep the victim warm with a blanket, jacket, or coat.
- ❑ Do not give the victim anything to eat or drink.
- ❑ Look, listen, and feel for breathing.
- ❑ Feel for a pulse.
- ❑ Control bleeding with direct pressure.
- ❑ Complete required reports.

Fire

First: Remove people from danger.

Second: Call 9-1-1.

Second: Contain spread of fire.

- ❑ Alert others in the area.
- ❑ Activate fire alarm or direct someone to do so.
- ❑ Dial 9-1-1 and provide the following information:
    - ❑ Exact location within the building—floor and room number
    - ❑ Type of fire, if known—electrical, wiring, paper, etc.
    - ❑ Your name and phone number including extension
- ❑ Evacuate to designated outdoor assembly area; follow evacuation procedures.
- ❑ Do not use elevators.
- ❑ Close all doors as you exit.
- ❑ Follow instructions of fire department officials and ERT.
- ❑ Remain at a safe distance from the fire and away from firefighting equipment.
- ❑ Do not reenter the building until public safety personnel say it is safe to do so.
- ❑ *Use a fire extinguisher only if you have been trained to do so.*
- ❑ Determine if it is safe, and fight fire only if:
    - ❑ Alarm has been sounded.
    - ❑ Fire is small and contained.
    - ❑ There is not a great deal of smoke in the area.
    - ❑ You have a safe egress route—reached without exposure to fire.
    - ❑ Available extinguishers are rated for size/type of fire.
- ❑ If in doubt, don't hesitate—evacuate immediately.
- ❑ Stand six to eight feet away from fire.
- ❑ When using a fire extinguisher, think P-A-S-S:
    - ❑ PULL the pin.
    - ❑ AIM the nozzle low at the base of the flames.
    - ❑ SQUEEZE the handle.
    - ❑ SWEEP side to side at base of fire.
- ❑ If the fire spreads, leave and close the doors.
- ❑ If clothing catches fire: stop, drop, and roll.

Building Evacuation

- ❏ Secure any sensitive documents or valuables.
- ❏ Power down or shut off computers and other equipment.
- ❏ Take all personal belongings and proceed to the assigned exit.
- ❏ Do not use elevators.
- ❏ Direct employees and visitors to the nearest exit.
- ❏ Keep to the right in hallways and stairways.
- ❏ Move quickly and quietly in order to hear emergency instructions.
- ❏ Proceed to your designated outdoor assembly area and check-in.
- ❏ Do not leave the assembly area until released.

Power Outage

- ❏ Take your flashlight.
- ❏ Calm staff and visitors.
- ❏ Discourage people from leaving the floor or the building unless instructed to do so.
- ❏ Power down computers and other equipment to avoid damage when power is restored.
- ❏ Wait for instructions from security, facilities, HR.

Bomb Threat

- ❏ Listen and do not interrupt.
- ❏ Keep caller on the line as long as possible.
- ❏ Note telephone number if available on phone LCD display.
- ❏ Complete the bomb threat checklist.
- ❏ If possible, alert a coworker to listen while the call is in progress.
- ❏ Make the following notifications or ask someone to do so:
  - ❏ 9-1-1
  - ❏ Security
  - ❏ Facilities/Engineering
- ❏ Do not discuss the call with others.
- ❏ Do not use walkie-talkies, cell phones, pagers that may detonate an explosive device, and do not allow others to do so.
- ❏ If directed to do so, evacuate; follow evacuation procedures.
- ❏ Do not touch, move, or handle any suspicious package or device.

Bomb Threat Checklist

Number at which call is received:	**Date:**	**Time:**

Length of call:	**Sex of Caller:**	**Age:**

Questions to ask:

Did you place the bomb?
Where has it been placed?
When will the bomb explode?
Why are you doing this?
What kind of bomb is it?
What does it look like?
What type of explosive was used?
What is your name?
What is your address?

Caller's voice:

accent	loud
angry	nasal
calm	normal
cracked voice	rapid
crying	raspy
deep	slow
deep breathing	slurred
excited	soft
familiar	stutter
lisp	whisper

What were the exact words of the threat?

Background sounds:

animal noises	music
clear	motor
factory machinery	office noise
house noises	pa system
long distance	phone booth
office machinery	static

Threat language:

foul	Message read (by
incoherent	threat maker)
irrational	Taped
	Well-spoken

Immediately report call to:

Name:
Position:
Phone number:

Notes:

Hazardous Materials Incident

If a hazardous material spill is observed in the building:

- ❏ Note any odor, visible gasses, or ill effects on people.
- ❏ Call 9-1-1.
- ❏ Report the following information:
    - ❏ Exact location within the building—floor and room number
    - ❏ Characteristics of the substance—solid, liquid, color, odor
    - ❏ Your name and phone number
- ❏ Advise facilities/engineering and security.
- ❏ Leave the area immediately and advise others nearby to do so.
- ❏ Restrict access to the area.
- ❏ Direct exposed persons to proceed to a safe area.
- ❏ Confine all exposed personnel in safe area; restrict contact with other persons.
- ❏ Close all doors.

If a hazardous materials incident is observed outside the building:

- ❏ Close all windows and doors.
- ❏ Dial 9-1-1 and provide the following information:
    - ❏ Location of the incident or source of the hazardous material, if known
    - ❏ Characteristics of the material—liquid, gas cloud, etc.
- ❏ Notify facilities/engineering and security.
- ❏ Public safety officials may advise of further actions to be taken, e.g., shelter in place.
- ❏ Remain inside the building until advised that it is safe to leave.

Workplace Violence

When threatened by an individual or witnessing a threat:

- ❏ Take all necessary precautions to assure your safety and the safety of others.
- ❏ Remain calm and nonthreatening.

❑ Do not attempt to call for assistance while talking to the person.

❑ If safe to do so, signal someone to 9-1-1 and security.

❑ Avoid any type of challenging stance.

❑ Do not talk with your hands; do not point at the individual.

❑ Speak clearly and calmly.

❑ Listen to what the person says; be supportive and understanding.

❑ Do not threaten, argue, or treat the individual in a disrespectful manner.

❑ When it is safe to do so, make all appropriate notifications, or signal someone to do so:

    ❑ 9-1-1

    ❑ Security

    ❑ HR

If a weapon is involved or if you think a weapon may be involved:

❑ Explain your movements at all times.

❑ DO NOT make any quick moves.

❑ If possible, signal for help.

❑ Speak softly and clearly; maintain eye contact.

❑ Cooperate fully with all demands.

❑ If the individual(s) demand money or other valuables, hand it over.

❑ Attempt to increase the distance between yourself and the individual(s).

❑ Do not try to grab the weapon or overpower the person.

❑ Withdraw if you have the opportunity to do so—quickly, quietly, and safely.

❑ When it is safe to do so, call 9-1-1.

❑ Provide as much information as possible:

    ❑ Your name and complete location information

    ❑ Injuries, if any

    ❑ The identity or description of the person(s) involved

    ❑ Last known location of person

❑ Follow all instructions given by law enforcement and security personnel

Terrorist Attack

- ❏ Follow all instructions given by public safety officials and government agencies.
- ❏ As directed, have facilities/engineering take the following steps:
    - ❏ Shut down HVAC.
    - ❏ Set up decontamination/wash-down stations.
- ❏ Restrict building ingress and egress.
- ❏ Listen to the radio for further information and updates.

In the event of a biological or chemical attack:

- ❏ Stay alert for attack warning signs. Early detection enhances survival.
- ❏ In any case of suspected exposure to chemical or biological agents, no matter what the origin, seek medical assistance as soon as possible, even if no symptoms are immediately evident.
- ❏ Move upwind from the source of the attack.
- ❏ If evacuation from the immediate area is impossible, move indoors and upward to an interior room on a higher floor.
- ❏ Close all windows and exterior doors.
- ❏ Shut down HVAC.
- ❏ Cover your mouth and nose. If gas masks or surgical masks are not available, use a handkerchief, coat sleeve, or a piece of clothing.
- ❏ Cover bare arms and legs; bandage cuts or abrasions.
- ❏ If splashed with an agent, immediately wash it off using generous amounts of warm soapy water.

Suspicious Mail or Package

If you receive a suspicious letter or parcel:

- ❏ Do not open or handle excessively.
- ❏ Direct all personnel in immediate area to move to a safe area.
- ❏ Dial 9-1-1 or direct someone to do so.

❑ Provide the following information:

  ❑ Exact location within the building - floor and room number

  ❑ Description of the letter or parcel

  ❑ Your name and phone number

❑ Do not hang up until told to do so by dispatcher.

❑ If opened, letters allegedly containing anthrax or another toxin should not be handled further.

❑ If there was a puff of dust or if particles fell from the envelope when it was opened, report that when assistance arrives.

❑ Wash your hands with soap and warm water.

❑ Make all notifications in accordance with emergency procedures and company policy.

❑ List all people who were in the room or area when the suspicious mail was recognized.

If a suspicious substance is released:

1. Leave the area immediately and advise others nearby to do so.

2. Restrict access to the area.

3. Direct exposed personnel to proceed to a pre-designated safe area.

4. Confine all exposed personnel in the safe area and restrict contact with other persons.

5. Dial 9-1-1 and describe the situation and the type of substance—powder, gas, liquid, etc.

Sheltering in Place

❑ Remain calm; calm others.

❑ Close all doors and windows.

❑ Close all window coverings and keep clear of windows.

❑ If the shelter in place order is in response to a civil disturbance, lock exterior doors.

❑ Do not use elevators.

❑ Do not leave the building or floor until authorized to do so.

❑ Follow instructions of fire department and other public safety officials.

❑ Remove those who are overly stressed and contact HR for assistance.

❑ Help with rumor control; disseminate information only when advised to do so.

❑ If shelter-in-place is ordered as a result of hazardous materials release, facilities/engineering may be advised to:

   ❑ Shut down ventilation.

   ❑ Shut down all heating and air conditioning.

   ❑ Seal exhaust fans, exhaust fan openings, and range vents.

Each organization is unique and varies from all others in a vast number ways—location, type of business, size, number of employees, and culture. As a result, emergency procedures must be adapted and tailored to best meet your organization's needs and current capabilities. While applicable to most workplaces, these checklists must be reviewed and revised as necessary.

TABLETOP EXERCISE GUIDE

A tabletop exercise is a planned activity that offers those with safety, security, and emergency response responsibilities an opportunity to "talk through" a response to a fictitious emergency. Exercise participants become better acquainted with emergency plans and procedures and practice team problem solving in a nonthreatening environment. Participants are presented with an emergency scenario and simulated situation and are encouraged to discuss decisions in depth. The emphasis is on slow-paced problem-solving rather than rapid, spontaneous decision-making. This type of exercise allows for mental role playing regarding actions to be taken in response to situations.

An exercise tests plans and procedures. It is not a test for participants. For participants an exercise is a learning experience, an opportunity to practice problem-solving skills, and a means of identifying needed plan improvements before an incident actually occurs. It also provides a team-building opportunity for those who will be involved in responding to a given situation and who may not work together on a day-to-day basis.

While conducting a tabletop exercise takes some planning, it does not disrupt normal business operations, can be scheduled around other work, and is economical. The process is relatively straightforward. Start by scheduling a two-hour block of time for the tabletop exercise. This allows for a short pre-exercise briefing, the actual exercise, and a debriefing immediately following the exercise. Arrange for a meeting location, e.g., conference room or training room, and for water, coffee, tea, and cold beverages to be available during the exercise. Notify all exercise participants, of the exercise date, time, and location. Advise them to bring their copies of emergency plans and procedures.

Here are the basic steps for conducting a tabletop exercise:

❑   A facilitator, sometimes referred to as the exercise coordinator, develops the scenario and conducts the tabletop exercise. The scenario should be realistic, something that could actually happen at that location.

❑   Participants are provided with a scenario containing a description of the event and any necessary background information.

❑   The facilitator/exercise coordinator presents the scenario events, and perhaps a little information about the results of the event, in chronological order. Enough details should be provided to give the scenario credibility.

❑   Using any existing plans and procedures, participants discuss how they would handle the situation.

❑   If necessary, the facilitator/exercise coordinator may ask specific questions to facilitate group discussion.

❑   At the conclusion of the exercise, a debrief is conducted with all exercise participants. The exercise coordinator leads a discussion to review the actions participants indicated they would take to respond to the scenario, to discuss alternative actions that may be appropriate, and to identify areas for improvement.

❑   Using the lessons learned from the exercise, make any necessary improvements in plans and procedures.

A similar process can also be used to develop new plans and procedures from scratch, to prepare to respond to new threats, or to process extensive revisions of existing procedures. Those who will be involved in responding to actual emergencies and disasters use the tabletop exercise process to identify the actions to be taken, notifications to be made, etc., as they work through the given scenario. The result is plans and procedures that are developed from a real world perspective and that "belong to" those who will be the responders when an actual event occurs. This process also provides participants with an opportunity to identify ways to mitigate against the threats presented in the scenario.

For each of the following scenarios (situations), discuss how you would respond. Analyze these situations and prioritize your response according to the likely impact on:

❑   People (employees, customers, all other stakeholders)

❑   Facilities (buildings, machinery, equipment)

❑   Operations (ability to deliver the organization's service or product)

Once you have concluded your initial assessment, determine a course of action:

❑ What notifications need to be made and by whom?

❑ What immediate actions should be taken and by whom?

❑ If your organization has emergency response teams, would they be activated?

❑ After initial notifications have been made and the first steps have been taken, what are the longer-term considerations?

❑ To what extent does the front desk have the authority to handle the situation?

Consider each of these scenarios as it relates to your organization, and ask the following questions:

❑ Has your organization experienced a similar event?

❑ If so, was the response appropriate and adequate?

❑ If not, could your organization experience a similar event?

❑ Does your organization have policies, procedures, and plans in place to address each of these emergencies, threats, and unexpected situations?

❑ Has the front desk been provided with sufficient direction and guidance to handle the situation?

❑ As necessary, have all employees been trained to respond to these situations?

After customizing the following sample exercise scenarios, use them to conduct tabletop exercises to either test your existing plans and procedures and train exercise participants or to help develop new procedures.

Tabletop Exercise Scenario 1

DATE: Actual Date

TIME: 10:45 A.M.

WEATHER: Actual Conditions

STAFFING: Actual

The morning has been an extremely busy one with a greater than usual number of visitors, consultants, and repairpersons approaching the front desk to register and be announced. In addition, a new company has moved into a nearby building and there is apparently some confusion about their address. As a result, people are entering your building and asking you for help in finding their way to the other organization's location.

As you look up to make sure everything is okay in the waiting area, you notice a package at the end of the front desk. No delivery service or individual has indicated to you that they were leaving a package and no one in the waiting area has knowledge of the package. The front desk has not received a call from anyone in the organization indicating that they are expecting a delivery. Looking at the package, which is about the size of a large shoe box, you note that the package has no postmark and no return address. It is wrapped in heavy brown paper and tied with heavy twine. The box is hand-addressed to the "Humane Resources Deportment" and marked "Confidential."

Tabletop Exercise Scenario 2

DATE: Actual Date

TIME: 10:45 A.M.

WEATHER: Actual Conditions

STAFFING: Actual

A nicely dressed woman approaches the front desk curtly asking to immediately see Karen Reed (head of HR). In response to your question as to whether she has an appointment, she responds that she does not have an appointment, but that it's important that she see Ms. Reed anyway. When you suggest she take a seat while you call Ms. Reed's office to let her know the woman here, she adamantly refuses saying that she prefers to wait right where she is. Upon calling Ms. Reed's office, you learn that the person is not expected. She is apparently an unsuccessful candidate for a position with the organization. Over the past two weeks she has repeatedly called Ms. Reed's office. Ms. Reed does not want to see the woman today or any other day.

You report that Ms. Reed is not available and cannot see the woman with a suggestion that she write Ms. Reed a note outlining the reason for her visit and requesting a meeting at a later date. The woman becomes belligerent. She insists that she must see Ms. Reed today and that she will not leave the building until that happens. For about fifteen minutes she sits in the waiting area with her arms crossed and a scowl on her face, only to again return to the front desk and demand in an increasingly loud voice to see Ms. Reed...now.

Tabletop Exercise Scenario 3

DATE: Actual Date

TIME: 1:15 P.M.

WEATHER: Actual Conditions

STAFFING: Actual

The lunch hour is ending and there is the usual heavy traffic near the front desk as people return from lunch and others arrive for early afternoon appointments. While doing your customary look around the entry area, you note an unfamiliar man standing in the waiting area. He has not yet approached the front desk, and you ask if you can help him. He responds that he is waiting for a colleague who is supposed to be at your building around 1:30 and that since the person has not yet arrived, he will just wait outside. He then walks toward the entry. As you are greeting and signing in a client who is there to see your organization's CEO, out of the corner of the eye you see the individual who first seemed to be leaving the building head toward quickly toward the elevator lobby. You excuse yourself and ask the person if you can be of help, but he continues without responding.

Tabletop Exercise Scenario 4

DATE: Actual Date

TIME: 7:30 A.M.

WEATHER: Actual Conditions

STAFFING: Actual

You are heading toward the building a half-hour early in order to prepare for what is expected to be a busy day at the front desk. Several important visitors will be arriving throughout the day, and a press conference is scheduled for 10:00 to announce the opening of a new regional office. You are the first to arrive, and as you approach the building you see water trickling from under the front doors, across the sidewalk, and into the street.

Entering the building, you find that the floor of the front desk area is wet. Upon conducting an initial assessment to find the source of the water, you discover that there is apparently a break in a water pipe on the second floor, and water is leaking from the second floor into the first floor.

Tabletop Exercise Scenario 5

DATE: Actual Date
TIME: 11:00 A.M.
WEATHER: Actual Conditions
STAFFING: Actual

A mail clerk attempting to find shipping documents for a carton meant for another company opens the box. Inside the box are several plastic bags containing a powdery substance. While removing one of the bags for inspection, the mail clerk rips the corner of the bag on a sharp edge of the box. The startled clerk drops the bag, showering the work area with the powder that is immediately dispersed into the building ventilation system. The clerk and two other employees in the immediate area are exposed to the powdery substance.

Tabletop Exercise Scenario 6

DATE: Actual Date
TIME: 3:00 P.M.
WEATHER: Actual Conditions
STAFFING: Actual

Located directly across the street from your building is the headquarters office of a company that is in the midst of a labor action. More than thirty people walk back and forth in front of the building carrying picket signs. In the past few days there have been periodic incidents of minor vandalism and intimidating behavior directed at anyone entering the company's building. The situation is being covered extensively by local media. A car carrying several protesters drives by and throws a firebomb at the entrance to the building. Police and fire personnel and paramedics arrive on the scene, put out the resulting small fire, give first aid for two minor injuries, and contain the area. The injured are transported from the scene. Emergency traffic and pedestrian onlookers have created a great deal of congestion in the area. Several employees are approaching the front desk to ask if they can go home early.

Tabletop Exercise Scenario 7

DATE: January
TIME: 2:30 P.M.
WEATHER: Heavy snow, high winds, temperature 25 degrees Fahrenheit
STAFFING: Actual

The area is experiencing a severe winter storm. In addition to the average number of employees in the building today, the front desk log indicates that four customers, a reporter from a business publication, and three contractors are in the building. With gale force winds and a continuing heavy snowfall added to earlier accumulations, roads into and out of the area have quickly become impassable. The highway patrol has asked announced that most roads are closed and that everyone should stay inside.

Weather reports forecast that the storm will continue for the next twenty-four hours. It is now expected that no one will be able to leave the building for as long as three days. Telephone and electric service within the area are intermittent.

Note: If you are not in an area that experiences winter snow storms, a rainstorm and high winds resulting in flooded streets and roads may be substituted.

Tabletop Exercise Scenario 8

DATE: Actual Date
TIME: 3:00 P.M.
WEATHER: Actual Conditions
STAFFING: Actual

Unknown to anyone in your organization, three weeks ago there was a change of tenants in a building about three blocks away. Until today no one in your organization was aware of the new tenant or of the fact that the company in question stores hazardous chemicals on site. An employee calls the front desk to report he has received a call from a friend from another organization in the area saying that there are several emergency units in the area. As you hang up, a uniformed officer wearing a gas mask approaches the front desk to report that there has been a spill of an unidentified chemical and that everyone in your building is to immediately shelter in place. No one is to leave the building, and there will be no access to the surrounding area until the spill has been contained, the substance has been identified, and any necessary clean-up is completed.

Tabletop Exercise Scenario 9

DATE: Actual Date
TIME: 1:45 P.M.
WEATHER: Actual Conditions
STAFFING: Actual

There are sounds of disturbance at the main entry and a man, pushing by others who are entering the building, walks toward the front desk. As he approaches, you think you recognize the man as the recently divorced husband of Susan Johnson, an accounts payable department employee. You have been made aware that the husband has behaved violently and threatened Susan in the past. The man is disheveled and smells of alcohol. Upon reaching the front desk, the man leans over the front desk and demands, "Get Susan Johnson out here. I want to talk to her. Do it now and you won't get hurt, and neither will she."

Tabletop Exercise Scenario 10

DATE: Actual Date
TIME: 5:25 P.M.
WEATHER: Actual Conditions
STAFFING: Actual

At the close of the business day, your organization is holding an open house in the front lobby to celebrate the retirement of an employee who is known and well-liked by everyone in the organization. Many employees are present including executives and upper-level managers, board members, the retiring employee's family members, prominent community members, and media representatives. The front desk, preparing to close for the day, answers the phone and hears: "Great party you're having. Because you didn't invite me, I planted a bomb in the building. It will make a grand finale to the evening."

Tabletop Exercise Scenario 11

DATE: Actual Date

TIME: 8:30 A.M.

WEATHER: Actual Conditions

STAFFING: Actual

It's a busy morning and there are several visitors in the front desk area when all the power goes out in the building. Tuning in to a local radio station on a portable radio, you learn that there is a major widespread power outage. Reports indicate that the power company is still investigating to find the cause of the outage. There is not yet an estimate of when power will be restored. The emergency generator has apparently malfunctioned and did not come on.

Almost immediately an employee from the accounting department comes to the front desk wanting to know when the power will come back on, what they should do, what's being done about this situation. You are aware that the accounting department staff has been working long hours this week to close the books for the quarter and to complete all related reports and paperwork. This is an especially important quarter for the organization, and a special board meeting is scheduled for three days from today.

Tabletop Exercise Scenario 12

DATE: Actual Date

TIME: 1:00 P.M.

WEATHER: Actual Conditions

STAFFING: Actual

An earthquake measuring 7.0 M on the Richter scale occurs on the Hayward Fault, and the ground shakes violently for 20 seconds. The entire Bay Area has been affected with moderate to severe ground shaking experienced over an area covering several counties.

Significant damage has occurred throughout the Bay Area; landslides occurred in the hills, multiple fires have broken out as a result of broken gas lines and downed power lines; and electricity and telephone service are out. Many masonry buildings in the surrounding areas have collapsed; high-rise buildings are damaged; and wood-frame homes have shifted off their foundations. All Bay Area bridges are closed due to damage to 'access roads; numerous streets throughout a three-county area are cluttered with debris and are impassable; and runways at all area airports are closed.

In our offices people have difficulty standing and many are thrown to the ground. Windows break; equipment and tall furniture topple over; items fall from shelves and tables. Computer terminals that have not been attached to desktops fall to the floor. Paintings fall from the walls in the main entry and reception area. Electrical power is interrupted and the emergency generators are powering the entire building. Due to the power outage, our phone system is not functioning, but phone service is not interrupted in the area. A fire alarm is sounding on the third floor. There are reports of minor structural damage to the Data Center and in the supply room.

There are no reports of severe injuries, though some employees have what first appear to be minor abrasions and cuts.

In the front desk area, while there is no apparent structural damage, a large planter has fallen over, paintings crashed to the floor, and magazines from a tabletop are scattered over the floor. Of the four visitors in the waiting area at the time of the earthquake the only injury appears to be an injured ankle suffered when the visitor fell during the earthquake's initial impact. Another of the visitors, however, is extremely frightened and is sobbing uncontrollably.

Aftershocks measuring 3.5 and 3.2 on the Richter scale occur within minutes following the first shock.

INTERNET RESOURCES

American Red Cross
Consult your phone directory for the local chapter.
http://www.redcross.org

Bureau of Alcohol, Tobacco, and Firearms (BATF)
http://www.atf.treas.gov

Canadian Red Cross
Consult your phone directory for the local chapter.
http://www.redcross.ca

Centers for Disease Control (CDC)
http://cdc.gov

Federal Bureau of Investigation (FBI)
http://www.fbi.gov

Federal Emergency Management Agency (FEMA)
P.O. Box 70274
Washington, DC 20024
To order publications: 800-480-2520
http://www.fema.gov

National Oceanic and Atmospheric Administration (NOAA)
http://www.noaa.gov

Occupational, Safety and Health Administration (OSHA)
http://www.osha.gov

Office of Critical Infrastructure Protection and Emergency Preparedness (OCIPEP)
http://www.ocipep.gc.ca

Office of Hazardous Materials Safety
http://hazmat.dot.gov

The U.S. Department of Homeland Security
http://www.ready.gov/index.html

U.S. Fire Administration (USFA)
http://www.usfa.fema.gov

United States Postal Service
http://www.usps.com

Most states, territories, and provinces have emergency management agencies, and the majority of these have Web sites that provide mitigation, preparedness, response, and recovery guidelines, tips, and pointers. In addition many local government emergency management agencies (counties, cities, and towns) also have Web sites that make specific local emergency preparedness information available.

INDEX

ABOUT THE AUTHOR

BETTY A. KILDOW is a sole proprietor consultant with more than twenty years of business management experience. A Certified Business Continuity Professional (CBCP) with the Disaster Recovery Institute International and a Fellow of the Business Continuity Institute (FBCI), Ms. Kildow has specialized in emergency management, disaster recovery, and business continuity consulting for more than fifteen years. She has managed emergency response and business continuity projects for a broad spectrum of businesses and public agencies. She is experienced in facilitating all related project phases and tasks...conducting hazard assessments and business impact analyses, developing plans and procedures, designing and delivering training programs, conducting program reviews and audits, planning and facilitating simulated disaster exercises and tests, and coaching those newly assigned to business continuity responsibilities.

An accomplished trainer, Ms. Kildow taught Introduction to Emergency Management at the U.C. Berkeley Extension from 1995 to 2001. Ms. Kildow developed a three-day business recovery seminar for the American Management Association International which she has delivered at locations throughout the U.S. for more than six years, both as a public seminar and as tailored on-site training.

Ms. Kildow has written articles that have appeared in professional publications, and she is often called upon as a speaker for meetings and conferences. She served as script and technical advisor to Commonwealth Films (Boston) in the production of "Ready for Anything," a business continuity video released in 2002.